A Gift For:

_____

From:

_____

Copyright © 2005 by Mark Gilroy Communications, Tulsa, Oklahoma

Published under license from J. Countryman®, a division of Thomas Nelson, Inc.

Managing editor: Jessica Inman

For a list of acknowledgments, see pages 254-255.

Unless otherwise indicated, Scripture quotations are taken from *The Holy Bible*,
New Century Version, copyright © 1987, 1988, 1991 by Word Publishing,
Dallas, Texas 75039. Used by permission.

Scriptures marked NKJV are taken from The New King James Version.
Copyright © 1979, 1980, 1982, Thomas Nelson, Inc.

Scripture quotations marked NIV are taken from the *Holy Bible*,
New International Version®. NIV®. Copyright © 1973, 1978, 1984 by International Bible Society.
Used by permission of The Zondervan Corporation. All rights reserved.

www.hallmark.com
www.jcountryman.com
www.thomasnelson.com

Designed by Thinkpen Design LLC, Springdale, Arkansas

ISBN #1404103473

Printed in China

SOUL MATTERS

MATTERS

for Moms

BOK4302

Contents

CONTENTS

Care for a Mother's Soul

What good is it for a mother to give the whole world to her children—but lose her own soul?

In our mad-dash, non-stop way of life, we too often forget about—or blatantly ignore—what matters most for our lives. But deep down, the simple truth that nothing—no achievements, no pleasures, no possessions—equals the value of the human soul, resonates in our inner being. Because what we most want for ourselves is to live our lives with significance and meaning. We long to be all that God created us to be.

If, as a mother, you have found yourself too busy and distracted with the hundreds of things that clamor for your attention to seek nourishment for your soul; if you have been simply going through the motions of fulfilling God's best plans for your life; if you are ready to stop floating with the currents of a shallow society in order to see a remarkable difference in your life—and profoundly impact the lives of your family and others around you—then *Soul Matters for Moms* is for you.

Soul Matters for Moms tackles the crucial life issues you face, weaving together poignant personal reflection questions, inspirational quotes, real life stories from others, God's promises, brief—but hard-hitting—Bible studies, practical life application ideas, and prayer starters to help you to discover for yourself how to let your soul take flight and soar!

The best and most beautiful things in the world cannot be seen or even touched. They must be felt with the heart.

HELEN KELLER

User's Guide

SOUL MATTERS FOR MOMS is easy to follow and use, but to maximize the benefit you get from this resource, here are a few quick ideas and suggestions for your consideration.

TO THINK ABOUT

In any area of study, when we understand how a topic relates to our specific circumstances, we experience increased levels of interest, comprehension, and retention. When you ask yourself the questions with each topic, take your time and reflect on recent events in your own life.

LESSON FOR LIFE

These quick, hard-hitting, to-the-point Bible studies are not designed to provide you with everything you need to know and "all the answers" on each of the topics, but they are designed to stimulate your own thinking and discovery learning. You will enhance what is provided here when you take the extra time to look up all the Bible passages that are referenced.

"God Will" Promises

One of the ways our souls take flight is when we truly believe in our hearts that God is good and faithful. These life-changing promises have been embraced and experienced by women of faith for centuries and have stood the test of time. When one of the promises is particularly relevant to your life, take a few extra minutes to memorize the verse so it will always be close to your heart.

REAL LIFE

True life stories are an inspiring way to see how God is at work in the life of others. Some of these stories will be exactly what you need to make some important life changes and decisions. But you don't have to relate to every single person's story to discover dynamics that will help you experience God's presence more fully in your life.

ACTION

Not every Action Step found in *Soul Matters for Moms* will be just right for you. But don't be afraid to stretch yourself and try something you would not normally think of on your own. Or let the ideas found with each soul matter prompt you to come up with an even better way to put truth into practice.

PRAYER

Let this brief prayer starter help you express your own requests, thanksgiving, and praise to God.

DEPENDING ON GOD

IN THE MIDST OF PRESSURES AND BUSYNESS, FIRM BELIEF IN A GOOD AND LOVING GOD IS THE ONLY ROAD TO VIBRANT LIVING.

I have been driven many times to my knees
by the overwhelming conviction that I had
nowhere else to go. My own wisdom, and that of
all about me, seemed insufficient for the day.

ABRAHAM LINCOLN

 ## To Think About

- Do you have confidence that God will take care of you and provide what you need—even when life is difficult?
- When things go your way, do you acknowledge that God is the giver of all good gifts?
- Do you ever wait for hard times to come before you to turn to God for help?

11

LESSON FOR LIFE

Promises

God will:

Hear your prayers

Psalm 18:6

Refine you

Zechariah 13:9

Give you refuge

Isaiah 4:5-6

Meet your needs

as you seek Him

Matthew 6:33

Strength Through Weakness

BIBLE STUDY PASSAGE: PHILIPPIANS 3:3-8

He chose what the world thinks is unimportant and what the world looks down on and thinks is nothing in order to destroy what the world thinks is important.

1 CORINTHIANS 1:28

Mother Teresa began her work as a nun teaching high school in Calcutta. But it was the dire plight of the children in the slums near the school that weighed on her heart. With zero funding and nothing but trust in God's call and providence, she founded an open-air school for the poorest children of the Calcutta streets. This tiny woman of faith showed the world what God can do through someone who totally trusts in Him.

Her daily prayer was one of great dependence: "Shine through me and be so in me that every soul I come in contact with may feel Thy presence."

In life, we tend to think everything is up to us. We want to be masters of our destiny and our every situation. But too often we discover that not all of life is under our control. A child's illness. An economic downturn. Conflict among neighbors. Too many poor orphans on the streets of Calcutta.

The good news is that with trust in God, we are never power-less or helpless. The Apostle Paul was a formidable character: He had his day's equivalent of two doctoral degrees (law and theology); he was a religious zealot who followed the letter of the law (Philippians 3:6); he came from a wealthy and influential family (Philippians 3:5). But it was when he discovered that all his efforts and abilities weren't enough that he truly became a powerful force for God. He helped launch the Christian faith and turn the world upside down.

That's why he was quick to say, "The less I have, the more I depend on Him" (see 2 Corinthians 12:10). That's why this great orator would point out, "My teaching and preaching were not with words of human wisdom that persuade people but with proof of the power that the Spirit gives" (1 Corinthians 2:4).

God has blessed you with gifts and talents to make a differ-ence in your world—including your family. But He's also created you with the need to depend on Him consistently.

Sometimes the greatest challenge in our lives is to not try harder but to trust more. ➔

But he said to me, "My grace is enough for you. When you are weak, my power is made perfect in you." So I am very happy to brag about my weaknesses. Then Christ's power can live in me.

2 Corinthians 12:9

 ## REAL LIFE

Don't Forget to Pray, Mommy

AUTUMN J. CONLEY

As a single mom working one and a half jobs just to keep the lights on and a little gas in the car, my life often feels like a three-ring circus. I don't mind the circus so much, but trying to be the ringmaster of all those rings at once can make my head spin.

On one of these manic, crazy-busy days, my bright seven-year-old reminded me that one thing that could have taken the sting out of the rush-bug was the first thing eliminated from my to-do list.

I had left the office in a hurry, trying to escape my ever-expanding inbox with some shred of sanity. I sped home, my mind frantically occupied with dinner to be made, newsletters to be typed, laundry to be done, posters to be created, homework to be reviewed, and lunches to be packed.

My daughter came wandering to the car when I got to the sitter's. I remember my mom accusing me of being "slower than Moses." I was convinced Moses could move faster than my daughter even if he was on crutches. As she piled her backpack, her muddy shoes, and herself into the backseat, I sighed, revved the engine, and said, "Mommy's in a hurry. Come on," in a frustrated huff. I suppose it would have taken too much precious time to say hi before I started grumbling.

"You're always in a hurry," she mumbled, looking out the window. I felt bad. But still I kept on rushing and huffing and sighing.

By ten that night, I was finally able to get around to prepping my daughter for bed—lucky her. I just knew that long after she had drifted into sleep with her stuffed hippo beneath her fluffy pink quilt, I'd still be awake, busily attending to details. I tucked her in, kissed her hastily on the forehead, and said goodnight.

She stopped me in my rushed tracks as I flicked off the Strawberry Shortcake light switch. "Mommy, make sure to say your prayers before you go to sleep," she soberly commanded. I was glad she reminded me, but embarrassed that she had to.

In my crazy task- and worry-filled day, I hadn't left room for the most important thing of all, and my daughter, as young as she was, had remembered something so much more vital than laundry and meetings and oil changes and spelling lists.

God tells us to "be still." I think He tells us this because He knows that our lives are not still, and it takes some effort on our part. It isn't always easy to set aside time to pray and commit my fast-paced life to God. But being still and soaking up His provision of wisdom and guidance is worth every effort. And, thankfully, even if I forget to put Him on my agenda, He always puts me on His. ➤

ACTION STEP

READ THROUGH HEBREWS 11 IN YOUR NEW TESTAMENT, WHICH PROVIDES A LIST OF OLD TESTAMENT CHARACTERS WHO COMPLETELY TRUSTED GOD— AGAINST ALL ODDS. NOW THINK OF THE TWO OR THREE MOST DIFFICULT MOMENTS IN THE LAST FEW YEARS OF YOUR LIFE. DID YOU FACE THOSE TIMES WITH FAITH IN GOD? IF NOT, HOW WOULD FAITH HAVE MADE A POSITIVE DIFFERENCE?

PRAYER

God, I give to You every difficulty, fear, and uncertainty—along with every success and good thing—and trust You to provide the strength and grace, the perspective and poise I need to depend on You in all the situations of my life.

SPECIAL MOMENTS

IN THE MIDST OF DAILY LIVING, WE NEED TO KEEP OUR EYES OPEN TO LITTLE EVENTS THAT MEAN A LOT TO OUR KIDS—AND TO US.

*When you look at your life, the greatest
happinesses are family happinesses.*

JOYCE BROTHERS

TO THINK ABOUT

- 🔑 What are some of the simple yet profound moments that have been important to you?
- 🔑 Do your children have a sense of wonder and appreciation?
- 🔑 How can you cultivate a spirit of wonder in your child's heart—and your own?

LESSON FOR LIFE

Promises

God will:

Do good things

in your life

Psalm 92:4

Give you joy through

your children

Proverbs 23:24

A Tale of Two Hearts

BIBLE STUDY PASSAGE: PSALM 40

Fill us with your love every morning. Then we will sing and rejoice all our lives.

PSALM 90:14

Though father and son, these two men had completely different outlooks on life.

David declared: "Many, O Lord my God, are Your wonderful works Which You have done" (Psalm 40:5 NKJV).

Solomon grumbled: "But then I looked at what I had done, and I thought about all the hard work. Suddenly I realized it was useless, like chasing the wind. There is nothing to gain from anything we do here on earth" (Ecclesiastes 2:11).

We often think of Solomon as the wisest man who ever lived because of his covenant with God: "God gave Solomon great wisdom so he could understand many things" (1 Kings 4:29). But Solomon's life is also a testament to folly. He said of himself: "So I decided to find out about wisdom and knowledge and also about foolish thinking, but this turned out to be like chasing the wind. With much wisdom comes much disappointment; the person who gains more knowledge also gains more sorrow" (Ecclesiastes 1:17-18).

We live in an overstimulated society, filled with nonstop entertainment, from music to videos to sports to video games. No wonder so many young people are bored—"There's nothing to do!"—and even cynical at an early age.

One of the great challenges of parenting today is passing on a spirit of wonder and appreciation to your children. There is no list of secrets and no shortcut. The only way to share it is to spend time with your kids and model awe, reverence, and joy of just how special life is.

One substitute that many parents try is to lavish more of everything on their children—more toys, trips, clothes, parties, and entertainment opportunities.

To recognize truly special moments, God moments, grace-filled moments, what we really need is less. A simple walk in the woods can do more for our—and our children's—soul than another trip to the amusement park.

In the words of Bill Copeland: "One of the wonders of life is just that—the wonder of life." ➡

I am very happy in the Lord that you have shown your care for me again.
Philippians 4:10

REAL LIFE

Today You Are Thirteen

SUE REEVE

My daughter's thirteenth birthday approached much too quickly. Despite my reluctance, I was soon to be a teenager's mom. The mere thought created angst!

"If only we were Jewish," I moaned to no one in particular, "we could celebrate a bat mitzvah"—that significant rite of passage bridging the often-turbulent chasm separating girl and woman. The special thirteenth birthday blowout I'd planned for my beloved daughter just didn't seem meaningful enough. Finally, I determined, I'd write a letter to this precious child, whom I knew must begin untying those apron strings sooner than I'd like.

"Dearest Angie," my letter began, "Today you are thirteen!" The ensuing paragraphs recalled the anticipation and wonder of her birth, the joy I'd felt watching her learn, grow, and blossom into lovely budding womanhood. I expressed fear of being mother to a teenager, a never-before-played role. I cautioned her to make wise choices, so aware that impetuous youthful passions can result in a lifetime of regrets. I wished her a life of lasting love. Carefully, I composed, edited, and typed motherly memories, hopes, and dreams for this elder daughter—joy of my heart.

On the eve of her landmark birthday, I finished the letter and signed it with "Mom" and a loopy heart. Very early in the morning I carefully folded the letter, slipped it into an envelope, wrote "Happy Birthday, Angie" on the front and quietly taped it to her bedroom door. Angie, with characteristic exuberance, upon discovering the letter, tore it from the door, read it on the run, burst into tears, and hugged me furiously, exclaiming, "Mommmm, that's soooo nice!"

Eight years later, I was composing a second "today you are thirteen" letter—this time to my equally precious younger offspring, Sarah. From birth, Sarah has exhibited a resolute and organized but quiet and gentle temperament. Upon finding her letter, my sleepy-eyed new teen slowly removed it from her bedroom door, carried it to the family room sofa, leisurely curling up in the corner. She neatly opened her birthday letter, Mom looking on in anxious anticipation. Carefully, my daughter digested her mother's heartfelt, love-filled wishes. Then, slowly, Sarah looked at me, and softly remarked, "That's nice, Mom."

Did my letters matter? I wondered. Months later, I realized that Sarah's had when I noticed the letter among a stack of papers on her desk, a sticky note affixed with her reminder, *Read this every year on birthday.* A few years later, I was helping Angie organize some linens following the birth of her first child. There lay her letter, neatly placed with other special mementos in the corner of her cedar chest.

How the years slip stealthily into yesterdays! So soon, I found myself grandmother to three amazing children, equally precious as their mommy and Auntie Sarah had been. In less than two years, my oldest will be a teenager, and already, I am beginning to mentally compose another "today you are thirteen" letter. ➤

ACTION STEP

AN OLD TRADITION AMONG AMERICAN CHURCHES THAT HAS BEEN LOST IS NOT SCHEDULING ANY ACTIVITY ON MONDAY NIGHTS, SO THAT FAMILIES COULD HAVE A SIMPLE EVENING TO BE TOGETHER TO PLAY GAMES. IT'S NOT QUITE SO SIMPLE TO SLOW DOWN THE DEMANDS FROM WORK, CIVIC CLUBS, SCHOOLS, AND YES, EVEN CHURCH, BUT CONSIDER ESTABLISHING YOUR OWN WEEKLY "FAMILY GAME NIGHT." IF YOUR KIDS ARE YOUNG, NOW'S THE TIME TO DO IT. IF THEY'RE TEENS, IT MIGHT BE A STRUGGLE, BUT LOOK FOR WAYS TO SIMPLY BE TOGETHER.

PRAYER

Father, help me teach my kids that life is a gift from You. Help us slow down, Lord, and hear Your voice.

SERVING OTHERS

TRUE HAPPINESS IS MEASURED
NOT BY WHAT WE HAVE,
BUT BY WHAT WE GIVE.

A little help is worth a great deal of pity.

ANONYMOUS

TO THINK ABOUT

- ☞ Who are people who have modeled a lifestyle of service for you?
- ☞ In what ways are you serving others today?
- ☞ What gets in the way of servanthood for you?

LESSON FOR LIFE

Promises

God will:

Bless you as

you bless others

Hebrews 6:10

Matthew 10:42

Use others to encourage

you and you to

encourage others

Acts 18:23

Be with you in the

presence of other

believers

Matthew 18:20

The Towel and Basin Society

BIBLE STUDY PASSAGE: JOHN 13:1-20

If I then, your Lord and Teacher, have washed your feet, you also ought to wash one another's feet. For I have given you an example, that you should do as I have done to you.

JOHN 13:14-15

Jesus' disciples seemed to wonder a lot about who was His favorite. In fact, two of the disciples, James and John, asked their mother to help them get the seats of honor in Jesus' kingdom. She asked Him: "Promise that one of my sons will sit at your right side and the other will sit at your left side in your kingdom" (Matthew 20:21).

Jesus' response was that she didn't know what she was asking. She and her sons were interested in the frills and benefits of power, but not the sacrifice involved. Otherwise, these sons of Zebedee could have been on Jesus' left and right when He prayed in the Garden (Matthew 26:40-46). Instead, they slept.

They could have been on His left and right when He was arrested (Mark 14:50). Instead, they fled.

They could have been on His left and right when He hung on a cross (Matthew 15:27, Luke 23:49, John 19:16-19, 26). Instead, they stayed quietly in the crowd.

When Jesus taught His disciples the true meaning of greatness, He taught with a towel and basin. He washed their feet—the duty of a house servant. Peter, still unable to comprehend the object lesson, initially refused to let Jesus lower himself in such a way.

We live in a competitive, self-aggrandizing world. Examples of humility, kindness, helpfulness, and caring for others first—servanthood—are hard to find. A lot of people are just out for themselves.

But the truth is that the happiest and most fulfilled people are those who follow Jesus as members of the "Towel and Basin Society." When we bless others, we are truly blessed in turn. ➤

Keep on loving each other as brothers and sisters.
Hebrews 13:1

REAL LIFE

Gifts of Love and Other Treasures

PATRICIA LORENZ

I've never had a friend whose child was a hospital patient. So I really didn't know what to expect when Andrew, my teenage son, was confined to the hospital for eleven long days. Andrew immediately requested no visitors or phone calls, so I launched into my mother mode of being the gauntlet that kept them all away.

I'd stay with him all day and evening, dash home at midnight, sleep for five or six hours, wake up without an alarm, write a daily update on my computer to friends and family, return voice mail messages, and get back to the hospital by 8 A.M. I stumbled around each time someone said, "What can we do to help?" My stock answer was, "Just pray for him."

By day four, our friends began to come up with ideas of their own. In the days that followed, I learned exactly what to do for someone whose child is in the hospital.

I learned from Rusty, who came over one afternoon with his lawnmower and mowed my entire yard, front, sides, and back. How he ever got through the foot-tall growth in the back yard is beyond me.

I learned from my friend Jean, who met me in the hospital cafeteria on her way home from work with a large chocolate malt and her listening ear for over an hour.

I learned from friends Sharon and Kay, who whisked me out of Andrew's room when he was sleeping and took me to the cafeteria for lunch. What bliss: women to talk to over nourishment.

I learned from Betsy, who showed up on warm and sunny day ten and drove me to a park and produced a three-course picnic, including fresh watermelon. It was a God moment.

I learned from Heather and Rusty's five-year-old, Hayley, who made me a bright, happy Mother's Day card which was waiting on my kitchen counter when I returned from the hospital at midnight the night before Mother's Day.

I learned from Ken, one of my son's nurses, who taught Andrew meditation for pain relief at 1:00 in the morning when Andrew couldn't sleep and Ken was on break.

I learned from my pastor, Father Tom, who not only spent hours with Andrew every single day in the hospital (the only visitor Andrew wanted) but who also stayed with him in our home the night he was released and I had to teach a class.

I learned that I will never, ever again do the usual, common things one does when a friend or a friend's child is in the hospital. No, I'll choose from the list of the most creative, most helpful gifts imaginable. God moments, every one of them. →

ACTION STEP

WHO DO YOU KNOW WHO NEEDS A HELPING HAND TODAY? A WIDOW?
SOMEONE WITH A SICK FAMILY MEMBER? PRAYERFULLY MAKE A LIST OF WAYS
YOU CAN BLESS OTHERS—AND THEN TAKE ACTION!

PRAYER

*Father, thank You for the people You've sent my way to bless me and help me
along when times were difficult. Show me who to reach out to today, Lord.
Amen.*

LOVING YOUR HUSBAND

ONE OF THE BEST WAYS TO EXPRESS LOVE TO OUR CHILDREN IS FOR US TO EXPRESS LOVE TO OUR HUSBANDS.

*Happy marriages begin when we marry the ones we love,
and they blossom when we love the ones we marry.*

TOM MULLEN

 TO THINK ABOUT

- ⚷ Why is it so difficult for so many couples to express love in their marriage?
- ⚷ What are your own challenges in giving and receiving love?
- ⚷ What are different ways an affectionate and loving couple can bless their children?

LESSON FOR LIFE

Promises

God will:

Bless your relationship as you adopt a loving attitude
Proverbs 17:9

Use your words to bless your husband
Ephesians 4:29

Perfect all virtues as you cultivate love
Colossians 3:14

Consider Others

BIBLE STUDY PASSAGE: PHILIPPIANS 2:1-11

Let each of you look out not only for his own interests, but also for the interests of others.

PHILIPPIANS 2:4 NKJV

Though psychological issues like self-awareness, self-esteem, and self-actualization are very important and all of us need to take good care of ourselves, it is easy to observe that many interpersonal and societal problems stem from a preoccupation with self. Nowhere is that more evident than in a marriage.

No wonder Paul's words to women—"submit to your own husbands, as to the Lord" (Ephesians 5:22 NKJV)—sound dissonant and abrasive in our modern culture. And no wonder his words to men—"love your wives, just as Christ also loved the church and gave Himself for her" (Ephesians 5:25 NKJV)—are equally dissonant and readily ignored!

If you are a single mom, don't think this soul matter isn't for you as well. All of us would do well to heed Paul's words: "Give more honor to others than to yourselves" (Philippians 2:3

NKJV). Again, his advice might make us cringe just a bit in our self-serving world, but his point is clear: Relationships require giving, loving, serving, unselfish individuals to thrive. The fact that it bothers many of us to "give more honor to others" is evidence of a soul condition of self-absorption.

It's obviously best when there are two partners ready to give of themselves humbly and freely, when a couple tries to out-give and out-bless one another. But sometimes one person has to break the cycle of self-interest and reach out to the other first with unconditional love. Remember, the context for Paul's words can be found a few verses later when he says of Jesus: "He did not think that being equal with God was something to be used for his own benefit. But he gave up his place with God and made himself nothing" (Philippians 2:6-7). Jesus becomes our model of love.

So how does loving your husband relate to being a mother? Simple. Since you will be your children's first and most profound teacher in life, how you model love and affection will shape their views of love and marriage. ➜

> Patience and
> encouragement
> come from God.
> Romans 15:5

REAL LIFE

Daddy's Lights

STEPHANIE WELCHER THOMPSON

It's about time, I thought as my husband dragged a ladder from the garage. Christmas Day was three weeks away. Michael had been promising to hang lights since Thanksgiving, but something always interfered—the weather wasn't right, he didn't feel well, or there was a football game on television.

When our two-year-old daughter heard the sound of aluminum scraping against brick, she ran to the front door. "Noise," yelled Micah.

I directed her into the dining room. We sat in front of the floor-to-ceiling windows and watched Michael go up, then down, and move the ladder again and again. Micah was mesmerized with the repetition. Each time Michael's feet hit the ground, Micah called, "Daddy!" like it was the first time she'd seen him all day. My husband played along, a surprised look on his face, waving like a lunatic.

Michael finished at dusk.

"Daddy home, Daddy home," shouted Micah as she raced to meet him.

"Wanna take a look?" he asked. The three of us held hands as we walked to the curb. White icicle lights gracefully hung from the guttering around our roof. A pair of illuminated deer grazed near the alpine spruce in the front flower bed. Green twinkle lights outlined the edges of the landscaping. Over the garage hung a three-foot evergreen wreath.

"Oh, honey! It's simply beautiful." I hugged Michael.

"Daddy, Daddy," Micah shouted, her tiny finger pointed toward the lights. Michael gave her a personal tour of the decorations, quietly explaining each one.

Several evenings later, I buckled Micah into her car seat to run an errand. It was dark as we pulled out of the garage, so the Christmas lights shined bright in our yard.

"Daddy, Daddy," shouted Micah when she saw the decorations.

"That's right," I confirmed. "Daddy decorated our yard."

We turned the corner and drove up the street.

"Daddy, Daddy."

I looked in the rear view mirror. Micah was pointing out the window. "No, Micah, that's not Daddy." I assumed the passing car had caught her attention.

We drove through the neighborhood and Micah continued calling for Daddy, her finger pointing toward the window.

I didn't respond this time, and she finally stopped once we were out of our subdivision.

On the highway, she did it again.

"Daddy, Daddy."

Instead of watching Micah in the rear view mirror, I looked in the direction she was pointing. She called to Christmas lights that circled a row of trees.

I finally understood. "No, baby. Daddy didn't hang those lights," I corrected her and laughed.

"Daddy, Daddy," she persisted.

The entire season, whenever we saw Christmas lights outdoors, Micah ➔

praised Daddy. That year, our preschooler taught me something. Instead of focusing on what my husband didn't do, I learned to compliment what he accomplished. Micah showed me the wonder of unconditional love by helping me see my husband through the eyes of his admiring daughter.

ACTION STEP

IN OUR CULTURE, IT IS ASSUMED THAT IT'S THE MAN'S JOB TO ASK THE WOMAN FOR A DATE. WHY NOT TRY A FUN ROLE REVERSAL AND ASK YOUR HUSBAND OUT FOR A DATE? BRING HIM FLOWERS AND CHOCOLATES AND PLAN A FUN EVENING.

PRAYER

God, thank You for my husband. Let me be a blessing to him today!

BLENDED FAMILIES

GOD LOVES TO BRING PEOPLE TOGETHER AND CREATE FAMILIES.

*It is not flesh and blood but the heart
which makes us fathers and sons.*

JOHANN SCHILLER

TO THINK ABOUT

- What are the greatest challenges in your blended family—or a blended family you are familiar with?
- What is the greatest joy in your family?
- What are the biggest obstacles to creating a blended family?

LESSON FOR LIFE

Promises

God will:

Be a Father to the

orphan and take

care of widows

Psalm 68:5

Give us the gift of love

Psalm 68:6

Adopt us as children

John 1:12

Making a New Family

BIBLE STUDY PASSAGE: RUTH 4:9-22

But he lifted the poor out of their suffering and made their families grow like flocks of sheep.

PSALM 107:41

Though all families have challenges, blended families often require even more work and patience due to dynamics like the pain of divorce, the challenge of shuttling between two households, the grief of a parent dying, the process of bonding with a new parent or child or sibling, or other matters of the heart.

The intensity of the challenges ranges from the amusing and humorous to the defiant and hurtful. But whatever your situation, and no matter what level of challenge is before you, consider these dynamics—

- All families have some conflict, and not everything need be "blended" in blending two families into one. So keep poise and grace under pressure—something all parents are required to do. "Do not become angry easily" (James 1:19).
- Relationship building takes time, which can extend well

into the adult years. The important thing is to move
your family in the right direction as you are able. If
others won't cooperate and sabotage your best efforts,
have peace knowing you've done your part. "Do your
best to live in peace with everyone" (Romans 12:18).

- Allow children to define the "bond" you experience.
  When you love a child with all your heart, it is natural to
  want him or her to reciprocate at the same level of inti-
  macy. But if you push too hard, you may lose the very
  thing you are most wanting—a mutual relationship of
  love and trust. "Love patiently accepts all things. It
  always trusts, always hopes, and always remains
  strong" (1 Corinthians 13:7).

- Thank God for your new family—no matter what is going
  on right now. One of the best ways to change circumstances is an attitude of gratitude. Begin to see what God
  is creating, not just what is in front of you now. "Faith means
  being sure of the things we hope for and knowing that
  something is real even if we do not see it" (Hebrews 11:1).

The good news is that you don't have to figure things out by
yourself. God—who loves to create families—will help you
each step of the way. ➤

You belong to
God's family.
Ephesians 2:19

REAL LIFE

Bonus Mom

JOANNE SCHULTE

"You don't love my family as much as you love yours and you don't treat us all the same."

This emotional outburst from my sixteen-year-old stepdaughter stopped me in my tracks. Where had these hurtful words come from? What had I done to cause her to be so upset with me that she would lash out in such anger? *Lord, help me.*

I was crushed, deeply hurt, and in complete disbelief that she would even confront me this way.

No doubt she resents me for marrying her father only a year after her mother passed away. And now she's part of a blended family of seven children. I realize it's a big adjustment for her, for all of us. Lord, what is in her heart? How can I reach her?

Days following her outburst, she was still withdrawn and not very communicative, but I could tell that her attitude had improved.

What had made her change? Had the outburst helped release her frustration with this new family arrangement—and with me? Whatever it was, I thanked the Lord.

I tried to get close to her, to at least be her friend. It was okay that she didn't call me Mom, as her younger brother and sister did. I knew I wasn't really the "wicked stepmother" that I felt like around her, but I wondered if she saw me that way.

By the time she went away to college, our relationship showed signs of progress. She married, began a family, and somewhere during that time became a Christian. Then one day, she took me by surprise.

"I'm sorry for the way I treated you when I lived at home. Please forgive me."

Tears filled my eyes as she spoke.

"Yes, of course I will," I said.

I asked her to forgive me for anything I might have done to hurt her. She couldn't respond, but with tears in her eyes, gently nodded her head yes.

We hugged for a long time.

This was the beginning of a relationship that would only become closer with time. Yet I sensed she still struggled with who I was to her. I was not her birth mother, although I had always done "motherly" things with and for her. She could introduce my husband and me as her parents, but I knew it was still difficult for her to introduce me as her mom. It didn't matter to me how she referred to me. Our relationship had improved so much that now we were friends, and I was more than content with that.

But just recently I was sitting with her in church. The pastor asked everyone to turn to their neighbor and share something for which they were thankful.

She turned to me, touched my arm, and said, "I'm thankful for—my bonus mom." →

ACTION STEP

RATE YOUR BLENDED FAMILY IN THE FOLLOWING AREAS:

MUTUAL RESPECT:

1 —————————————————————10

STRENGTH:

1 —————————————————————10

ENJOYING ONE ANOTHER:

1 —————————————————————10

AFFECTION:

1 —————————————————————10

CONFLICT MANAGEMENT:

1 —————————————————————10

SHARED VALUES:

1 —————————————————————10

WHAT ARE SOME AREAS TO WORK ON AND PRAY ABOUT? WHAT ARE SOME AREAS TO THANK GOD FOR BLESSING YOU WITH?

PRAYER

Father God, thank You for the family You've given me. Please give my family grace, peace, and love, and guide us close to You.

ADOPTION

THE WORK AND TEARS AND WAITING INVOLVED WITH ADOPTION REFLECTS GOD'S LOVE IN ADOPTING US AS HIS CHILDREN.

*Adoption is when a child grew in its
mommy's heart instead of her tummy.*

AUTHOR UNKNOWN

TO THINK ABOUT

- What was the hardest thing you've ever had to wait for?
- Have you experienced a time of despair when you weren't sure of God's plan for you?
- Whether or not your children are adopted, do you take time each day to thank God for these precious gifts to you?

LESSON FOR LIFE

Promises

God will:

Adopt your child

and you as His own

Romans 8:15

John 1:12

Use all circumstances

for your good

Romans 8:28

Bring your life

satisfaction and

purpose

Psalm 37:4-5

Hold On

BIBLE STUDY PASSAGE: GENESIS 50:15-26

… let us run with perseverence the race marked out for us.

HEBREWS 12:3

God promised to make Abraham the father of a great nation, with descendants as numerous as the stars in the sky (Genesis 15:5). Despite his great faith, can you blame him for questioning when this was going to happen when he was still fatherless at age seventy-five (Genesis 12:4)?

Samuel anointed David as king of Israel in response to Saul's spirit of disobedience (1 Samuel 16:1). The problem is David was hunted like a fugitive and animal for the next seven years (1 Samuel 19:9). No wonder he cried to God, "Why have you forgotten me? Why am I sad and troubled by my enemies?" (Psalm 42:9).

Moses led the Hebrew slaves from captivity and into the Promised Land—over the course of forty years (Exodus 16:35). Jesus spent the first thirty years of His life as a child, son, student, brother, and carpenter before the right moment came for Him to begin His ministry (Luke 3:23).

Why doesn't God just bring about His plans in our lives right now? Could it be that one of the most important ways God forms us into the image of His Son Jesus Christ is through allowing us to express our faith in Him through waiting?

In the Proverb, Solomon points out the natural truism that "it is sad not to get what you hoped for. But wishes that come true are like eating fruit from the tree of life" (13:12). But Paul's testimony that "the sufferings we have now are nothing compared to the great glory that will be shown to us" (Romans 8:18) is a powerful reminder that God may not be early—but He's always right on time with just what we need.

You may be near the point of despair in some area of your life, but don't forget: God is your Father. He loves you and has good plans for your life. As difficult as it may be for you to wait for a child or for a conflict to resolve or for a better financial situation, remember that God went to great lengths to make you His child. And that is beautiful proof of His faithfulness. ➤

The Father has loved us so much that we are called children of God. And we really are his children.

1 John 3:1

REAL LIFE

The Waiting Game

KATHRYN LAY

"It's not fair," I yelled, throwing the pregnancy test across the room.

Another negative result. All around me our friends and relatives were having first, second, and even third babies. Yet no matter how hard I prayed and dreamed, I could not seem to get pregnant.

Finally, after ten years of trying and a false pregnancy that hurt us as if we'd truly lost a child, I became angry at God, the world, and myself. Every Mother's Day was torture. Every November 2, the due date of my "imagined" baby, I cried.

"It's never going to happen," I told my husband in despair. "Michael or Michelle won't be a part of our lives. I just don't have any more faith about this."

But no matter how much I pretended, I was hurting. I couldn't imagine life without children of our own, but I had given up all hope.

I mourned for my lost dream of motherhood. I knew we would have been good parents. Richard would have been an amazing father, I was sure of it.

Then an old friend called to tell us they'd just finished a parenting program with the state and had been approved to be adoptive parents.

Could this be the answer to our dream too?

Part of me wanted to ignore the possibility—I couldn't stand the thought of being disappointed again. But Richard and I talked it over and felt hope returning. We had to try.

We prayed.

Six months later, after parenting classes once a week, more paperwork, physicals, and home visits, we were approved to be adoptive parents. I couldn't stop smiling.

Five more months of waiting and calling our caseworker left me frazzled. We took more parenting classes in anticipation.

Then, on November 2, we received the call that changed our lives. We had a daughter waiting. Nine months old. Born with drugs in her system to a mother who mentally could not care for her, God knew she needed a home with parents who would love her completely.

"Her name is Michelle," our caseworker told us. I clutched the phone and forced myself not to scream into her ear. We had never told her we'd intended to name our first child Michael or Michelle.

Her name was proof of God's love for us. And that the call came on November 2, five years to the day of my "due date" from a false pregnancy, showed me how strongly God cared about the details of our joy.

And when we saw her, we quickly fell in love with this smiling, active, outgoing child. Now, more than thirteen Mother's Days later, I am amazed at how the darkest time of my life led up to the daughter I'd long dreamed about.

And now, my cup runneth over. My Michelle, the daughter of my heart. She was worth the wait. ➡

ACTION STEP

TAKE SOME TIME TODAY TO CELEBRATE THE DAY YOU BECAME GOD'S CHILD. IF YOU HAVEN'T ALREADY DONE SO, WRITE OUT YOUR TESTIMONY—THE STORY OF YOU COMING TO HAVE A RELATIONSHIP WITH GOD. TUCK IT INTO YOUR BIBLE TO READ AS A REMINDER OF GOD'S GOODNESS AND KINDNESS IN YOUR LIFE.

PRAYER

Father, I know You have good plans for me. Help me trust and lean on You today, and give me the patience I need to rest in Your plan.

TRAGEDY

NONE OF US ARE IMMUNE FROM
TRAGEDY, BUT WE HAVE THE PROMISE
AND HOPE OF A GOD WHO IS WITH US
IN THE MIDST OF ANY SORROW.

*In the night of death, hope sees a star, and
listening love can hear the rustle of a wing.*

ROBERT INGERSOLL

TO THINK ABOUT

- What is the most painful situation you have faced in your life?
- Who is someone you have seen overcome tragedy? What was their secret?
- What can you do right now to prepare yourself to meet any challenge you face in life?

LESSON FOR LIFE

Comforted Comforters

BIBLE STUDY PASSAGE: 2 CORINTHIANS 1:2-7

He heals the brokenhearted and bandages their wounds.

PSALM 147:3

Grief, heartache, and sorrow are a part of life. Death. Pain. Loss. Separation. It can be no other way, for if we care about and love someone or something in a way that creates joy, then that same care and love for the person can be turned to sorrow in the face of loss.

Though we can talk about certain stages of grief—denial, anger, bargaining, depression, acceptance (first presented by Elizabeth Kubler-Ross in the book *On Death and Dying*)—there is no set timetable or "cure" for grief. The stages can occur in any variety of sequence, and certain stages may recur and dominate what we are feeling.

The good news is that the God of "all comfort" meets us right where we are. He doesn't ignore our tears, grow impatient with our questions, or condemn us for feelings of anger. He doesn't demand that we "get over it and move on" at some proscribed time. But He does embrace us and cry with us and nurse us back to health and wholeness. God knows the hurt of rejection and the horror of losing His only begotten Son on a cruel cross.

And the comfort He gives to us enables us to comfort others (2 Corinthians 1:4). It doesn't mean we are suddenly wiser and have more words to share—sometimes all a person who is grieving wants is your presence and a shoulder to cry on.

We may never understand why suffering occurs, but we can receive the tender love and compassion of God. And we can hold to the promise of a heavenly home where there are no more tears and sorrow (Revelation 21:4). ➤

You have recorded my troubles. You have kept a list of my tears. Aren't they in your records?

Psalm 56:8

REAL LIFE

When God Became My Husband and Father

CINDY WALKER AS TOLD TO JESSICA INMAN

Buz reached back and patted my leg and told me he loved me. It was near the end of our four-day motorcycle trip, and I was tucked behind him on the powerful Honda cruising bike. I squeezed him back hard and savored the feeling of being close to him.

Twenty minutes later I looked around him and saw a gray car pull in front of us on the highway. As if watching everything in slow motion, I knew that what was about to happen would change my life forever.

I remained conscious through the accident and its aftermath, a hot whirlwind of metal and asphalt and searing pain. The next hours were chaos as bystanders sobbed and prayed and firemen and paramedics disentangled our broken bodies. An emergency medical chopper rushed Buz and me to the nearest hospital capable of dealing with our traumas.

When I woke after several hours of surgery to insert a titanium rod and repair trauma in my leg, as well as a cracked pelvis and kneecap, my first thought was on how Buz was doing. He was the rock in my life, and I knew I would lean on him as never before to get better. But the news wasn't good. He was in a coma, suffering from internal injuries, including possible brain damage. We prayed, knowing God could work a miracle.

But on Sunday, more than a thousand people gathered for a pastor's funeral. My pastor and husband's funeral. On Monday, I buried my soul mate and the father of my three daughters.

After the funeral, my soul-battered family stumbled into our season of recovery. Friends graciously moved in to take care of me, and we made a decision my two older girls would return to college, where they finished their semester in a state of blessed numbness. My youngest daughter, then only twelve, was used to spending hours each day with her daddy. She was so hurt and so furious that he was gone—and that she was stuck with me.

Meanwhile, my own grief consumed me, and I was in the midst of a long, slow recovery process, making it hard to focus on my children's needs. As family members and youth workers and neighbors surrounded us, I realized almost daily how much I'd depended on Buz.

In the months that followed, I finally began to allow myself to remember the details of the trip and the accident. There was no magical moment that took away my heartache—it's still there today—but I became deeply aware of God's love and faithfulness. He made my last weekend with my husband romantic and wonderful—as we rode together and stayed in quaint, funky inns, He showed me different signs, like the word *love* splashed big on the side of a speeding bus, prompting me to celebrate the love in my life. He sent people to comfort me after the accident. He helped my daughters where I couldn't and met our financial needs.

I had hidden behind Buz for so long. When he died, I needed God to be my everything—and I found that He would be. He became a Husband and Father to me and my family.

Five years later, my youngest and I have grown incredibly close—she's not just stuck with me anymore. Sometimes she comes in and just flops on my bed while I read, which I find delightful. I still ache for a reassuring hug from Buz— no one will ever love me the way he did. When my daughters face struggles in their lives, I desperately wish their father was here to comfort and advise them. But I've seen again and again that God is faithful to us. And His faithfulness is truly enough.

ACTION STEP

A WILDLY POPULAR SONG BY TIM MCGRAW INCLUDES THE LINE, "SOMEDAY I HOPE YOU GET THE CHANCE TO LIVE LIKE YOU WERE DYING." THOUGH WE CAN'T LIVE IN FEAR AND ANTICIPATION OF SAD TIMES, WE CAN FACE LIFE WITH THE SENSE OF THE IMPORTANCE OF EACH DAY. IF TODAY WAS YOUR LAST DAY TOGETHER, WHAT WOULD YOU SAY TO YOUR CHILDREN? TO YOUR SPOUSE? USE TODAY TO LET THEM KNOW HOW PRECIOUS THEY ARE TO YOU. DON'T PUT IT OFF.

PRAYER

Lord, protect my heart during tragedy—let me be drawn closer to You instead of away from You. Thank You for the extra strength and grace You give to face hard times.

BLESSINGS OF A MOTHER

LOVING OUR CHILDREN BRINGS SPECIAL JOYS AND IS ONE OF THE CLEAREST WAYS WE BECOME MORE LIKE JESUS.

Being a full-time mother is one of the highest salaried jobs in my field, since the payment is pure love.

MILDRED B. VERMONT

TO THINK ABOUT

- What do you enjoy most about being a mom?
- Do you take time to notice the small joys that come with interacting with your kids?
- What are some ways God uses children to bless their parents?

LESSON FOR LIFE

Promises

God will:

Bless your children

through you

Psalm 37:26

Bless you through

your children

Proverbs 31:28

Proverbs 23:27

Give you joy

Psalm 28:7

Blessed Is She

BIBLE STUDY PASSAGE: LUKE 1:42-55

But we were very gentle with you, like a mother caring for her little children. Because we loved you, we were happy to share not only God's Good News with you, but even our own lives. You had become so dear to us!

1 THESSALONIANS 2:7-8

When Paul wrote his letter to the church in Thessalonica, he could think of no greater way to describe his love for the people than to compare it to the love a mother has for her children. Not only was he gentle as their leader, but he loved them so much he poured his very life into them. What better description of a mother's love is there?

All who birthed a child understand full well that there are challenges to being a parent. Children can be difficult and needy. No wonder Paul considers the greatest character trait of a Christian to be love, and goes on to describe it terms and phrases like "kindness," "not self-serving," "not easily angered," "always protects," and "always hopes" (see 1 Corinthians 13).

In some cases, children are difficult because they are

needy and fragile. The good news is that God bestows special strength and comfort to those who comfort others—like the mother who comforts her child. (See 2 Corinthians 1:2-5.)

But at the end of the day, as you pour your life into your children, know that a special blessing from God awaits you. May you hear in your heart what was said of Jesus' mother: "Blessed is the mother who gave you birth and nursed you" (Luke 11:27 NKJV). ➤

Her children rise up and call her blessed.

Proverbs 31:28 NKJV

REAL LIFE

Home Alone

NANCY SIMMONS VINEYARD

Worry lines creased my boss's forehead as he stood in front of my desk. "We're adding another argument to our brief. Plus all the discovery documents are due tomorrow." He shifted his weight forward. "Looks like a long night ahead."

I forced a smile. "Okay." My job usually didn't require much overtime, but this case proved to be an exception.

Picking up the phone, I called my fifteen-year-old son, Brad. "Looks like I'll be home extra late tonight. Fix yourself a sandwich, honey. I'll call you later."

"Okay."

"Don't forget to do your homework. And don't have any friends over."

My son chuckled. "Mom, don't worry."

Easy for him to say, I thought. Since my husband worked nights, I did worry about leaving Brad by himself. He wasn't a troublemaker, but he lacked motivation when it came to his homework. And Brad was a typical teenager who loved to get together with his friends and turn up the volume on the stereo.

I refocused on the papers in front of me. About 8 P.M., I called Brad to tell him I still had a stack of documents on my desk to revise. Then I slipped back into the world of discovery documents and briefs that were anything but brief.

Later, the ring of the phone startled me.

"It's 9:30," said Brad. "When are you coming home?" His voice sounded as tense as my muscles felt.

"Pretty soon, I hope. I'm almost done with this document. And I'll call you right before I leave. Don't worry." I smiled at that thought as I hung up the receiver. *My son is worried about me? That's a refreshing change.*

Finally, Harry pronounced the documents done with no more revisions needed. Sighing with relief, I grabbed my coat and headed for home. A few miles down the road, it dawned on me. *I forgot to call Brad! What kind of mom forgets to phone home?* I wondered.

Our house looked dark from the street. I opened the door to a home that seemed as quiet and lonely as an abandoned playground. I hurried down the hallway to Brad's room. But there was no one in his bed. I flipped on the light switch. "Brad? Are you home?" No one answered.

Panic filled my body like a fire engulfs a building. I prayed for calmness, then walked back through the kitchen and into the living room, calling my son's name.

A groan came from the couch as I turned on a lamp on the end table. My son stretched, blinked, and frowned. "It's about time you got home. Now I can go to bed."

It was my turn to chuckle. I thanked the Lord for a son who cares enough to *try* to wait up for his mom. →

ACTION STEP

WHAT IS ONE SIMPLE, TANGIBLE THING YOU DO WITH YOUR CHILDREN THAT SHOWS THEM HOW MUCH YOU REALLY LOVE THEM? BAKE COOKIES? READ AN EXTRA-LONG STORY? DO AN ART PROJECT TOGETHER? IF POSSIBLE, FIND A TIME TO DO THAT IN THE NEXT TWENTY-FOUR HOURS.

PRAYER

O God, don't let me ever take for granted the blessing You have given me in my children. Grant me the strength and peace to build a love for You in their lives.

SPECIAL NEEDS CHILDREN

JESUS IS PRESENT AND CAN BE SEEN IN THE FACE OF A CHILD WITH SPECIAL NEEDS.

Whether we can walk or not, whether we can sing or not, whether we can create great works of art or simply manage play-dough, whether we can solve complicated mathematical equations or not, whether we can obtain our Ph.D. or merely complete vocational training, our value is still the same. Be certain that in the eyes of our Maker, we are equally precious and valuable.

AUTHOR UNKNOWN

TO THINK ABOUT

- What are the extra challenges you have experienced—or seen other mothers experience—with special needs children?
- What are the extra joys that come with special needs children?
- How can you draw closer to God through your love and compassion for a special needs child?

LESSON FOR LIFE

Promises

God will:

Give you strength
Philippians 4:13

Increase your love
1 Thessalonians 3:12

Help you know
what to do
James 1:5
Proverbs 3:5-6

Care for you
1 Peter 5:7

The Face of a Child

BIBLE STUDY PASSAGE: MATTHEW 5:1-10

At that time Jesus said, "I praise you, Father, Lord of heaven and earth, because you have hidden these things from the people who are wise and smart. But you have shown them to those who are like little children."

MATTHEW 11:25

In God's economy, the world's value system often gets turned upside down!

- There is strength in weakness (2 Corinthians 12:10).
- There is wealth in poverty (Luke 6:20).
- There is peace in the midst of storms (Philippians 4:7).
- There is greatness in servanthood (Matthew 20:26).
- There is supernatural comfort in the midst of tragedy (2 Corinthians 4:9).

And mothers who have special needs children discover there is a special wisdom and an indefatigable joy present in the life of God's cherished little ones.

One of the great challenges of being a mother to a special needs child is our society's obsession with perfection. Popular images of beauty and success hurt many people in their self-image and confidence, so we shouldn't expect it to be much different with having a special needs child. But God's answer to the world is: "People look at the outside of a person, but the Lord looks at the heart" (1 Samuel 16:7).

The greatest joy in having a special needs child—with and beyond the special love you feel as a mother—is that Jesus can literally be seen and found in the face of those people who have a variety of needs. Jesus himself said to His followers: "Anything you did for even the least of my people here, you also did for me" (Matthew 25:40). Isn't it wonderful to know that when you as a mother care for and protect the soul of your child, God cares for your soul in a special way at the same time? ➡

He does not enjoy the strength of a horse or the strength of a man. The Lord is pleased with those who respect him, with those who trust his love.

Psalm 147:10-11

REAL LIFE

The Heart of an Angel

SHERI PLUCKER

I forced my eyes shut in shallow, restless sleep. Our scheduled day of delivery had caused nervous anxiety as I prayed to God, "Please protect our baby girl during the delivery."

Later, my eyes opened and I glanced at the alarm clock. 6:00 A.M. I shuffled into the bathroom to turn on the shower. The hot water soothed my fatigued body as I whimpered with tears, calling out for God to perform a miracle on our unborn child and cure her of Down syndrome.

I remembered when I breathlessly answered the phone and heard my doctor say softly, "Your test was positive for Trisomy 21." My hand began quivering. Then there was silence, and I dropped the phone. Our two sons were horrified by my cries and quickly ran up the stairs to hug me. I'll never forget the comfort they gave.

In the months that followed, worrying about our unborn child and her safe arrival into this world had drained me physically, mentally, and emotionally. Now it was time to release the worries and concentrate on our future as parents.

Several hours later, I was holding my new daughter, and as I gazed at her precious face, I knew that many challenges lay ahead of us—but I would be proud to be the parent of this sweet child with Down syndrome.

The challenges came right away. Shortly after arriving home, I struggled to feed her three ounces of formula in an hour. After a series of tests and continued decline in appetite, she underwent her first open-heart surgery at only three and a half months old. Over time, it became apparent the surgery was unsuccessful.

We scheduled her second surgery at a children's hospital in Seattle. We knew her life was at risk as we waited for the surgical team to arrive. I squeezed Hailey close as tears pooled in my eyes. I pleaded with God, "Please protect our little girl."

Moments later, the anesthesiologist lifted Hailey from my arms and faded in the distance. I mumbled between sobs, "I'll see you soon," as my heart melted. The Lord reminded me as He had many times before that Hailey's life was in His hands. My part was to trust in Him.

Three hours and thirty-four minutes later, the surgeon stepped off the elevator and said, "Hailey's surgery was successful!" This time there were tears of joy.

Six days later, we were released from the hospital with a healthy daughter prepared to take on the world with her spunky personality.

Hailey is now five years old. We visit the cardiologist every six months for an update on her leaky mitral valve. We have become familiar with the unique pain and fear felt by special needs parents. But daily, we give thanks for the gift that was delivered to our family for a reason: to touch the lives of others with her captivating smile, laughter, and love that takes your breath away. Truly, I believe, Hailey has the heart of an angel. ➤

ACTION STEP

IF POSSIBLE, VOLUNTEER TO SPEND A DAY HELPING SOMEONE WITH A SPECIAL NEEDS CHILD, RELIEVING SOME OF THEIR EXTRA WORK. THIS MAY BE HARD FOR YOU, BUT FOCUS ON BLESSING THE CHILD AND THEIR PARENT OR CAREGIVER AND LEARNING AS MUCH ABOUT SPECIAL NEEDS CHILDREN AS YOU CAN.

PRAYER

Father, thank You that You love all children. Help me reflect Your mercy and compassion today.

CARING FOR AN AGING PARENT

CARING FOR CHILDREN AND PARENTS AT THE SAME TIME REQUIRES COMMITMENTS, BUT ALSO HOLDS SPECIAL BLESSINGS.

If you find it in your heart to care for somebody else, you will have succeeded.

MAYA ANGELOU

 TO THINK ABOUT

- What are some of the challenges of watching your parents age?
- Have you experienced any "role reversals" with your parents?
- Does our society adequately care for aging adults?

LESSON FOR LIFE

Promises

God will:

Reward your compassion

Matthew 25:40

Give you strength

Isaiah 40:31

Bless your parents and

children through you

Proverbs 17:6

Honor you in old age

Proverbs 16:31

Whither Thou Goest

BIBLE STUDY PASSAGE: RUTH 1

Love each other deeply with all your heart.

1 PETER 1:22

One of the most oft-cited verses in wedding ceremonies is found in the book of Ruth: "Don't beg me to leave you or to stop following you. Where you go, I will go. Where you live, I will live. Your people will be my people, and your God will be my God" (Ruth 1:16). The verse isn't exactly about marital love, nor does it refer to caring for a parent in need, but it is a marvelous example of commitment that is relevant to all relationships.

During an economic downturn in Israel, a woman named Naomi and her husband, Elimelech, moved to the neighboring kingdom of Moab in order to find work. She bore two sons, but tragically, Elimelech died, leaving Naomi as a relatively young widow.

In a series of events reminiscent of the book of Job, both of Naomi's sons, married to Moabite women, died, leaving a small family of three widows. Naomi determined it was time to return to her home of birth, Israel. She encouraged her two daughters-in-law to return to their roots and rebuild their lives. One, Orpah, did stay in Moab. But Ruth, in a beautiful expression of love and devotion, said: "Your God is my God."

Ruth's faithfulness to Naomi was indeed rewarded. God provided her with a husband in Israel, and she became an ancestor to both David and Jesus. Likewise, your faithfulness to your parents will bless your life as well.

In the Ten Commandments, only one of the commands explicitly states a blessing: "Honor your father and your mother so that you will live a long time in the land that the Lord your God is going to give you" (Exodus 20:12).

Though such commitment is barely acknowledged in our self-absorbed generation, be assured that God will provide you with the strength you need to be a blessing in your world. ➡

I have fought the good fight, I have finished the race, I have kept the faith. Now, a crown is being held for me— a crown for being right with God.

2 Timothy 4:7-8

REAL LIFE

The Caregiver's Crown

KATHERINE J. CRAWFORD

The week before Mother's Day, my sister said, "If I'd been thinking, I would have called Oprah. Mom would have made her show for sure. After all, how many women do you know who are eighty-three years old and taking care of their mother?"

It's true that several members of our family help make decisions for Grandma, and Mom's siblings often give her a break with daily care needs, but currently Mom is the primary caregiver for the woman she has known as Mama since she was six. Grandma is now ninety-seven.

Each morning, Mom and Grandma drive to Burger King or the Virginia Street Diner for breakfast. The servers know them well.

At least once a week, Mom prepares a picnic lunch and the two drive forty-five minutes north to the elk game reserve. While they eat, they use the binoculars and sight out the big elk, like the ones Grandma hunted years before.

The frequent phone calls between Mom and me are filled with news about what they ate together, where they went on their latest trip, and how she keeps Grandma occupied.

"Mama sat by the puzzle table today and sorted the colored puzzle pieces into piles," she said recently.

Last fall I received my "Bill of Rights" from Mom. She had recycled an old manila folder into a greeting card, gluing thirty-eight typed lines across it and adding her own wisdom between the lines by hand. One typed line said, "You have the right to laugh." Mom wrote: "And laugh and laugh."

After my coworkers applauded the clever card, I called Mom. "Where did you get the Bill of Rights?"

"From a Burger King place mat. Mama cut out all the lines. She did well, don't you think?"

My Bill of Rights is far better than an expensive card. It's a keeper. Mom's creativity gave the two an activity for the day and my friends and me a lot of laughter. I especially loved the line that said, "You have the right to put a paper crown on your head." Mom wrote: "And be queen for a day."

If I lived closer to Mom, I'd place a caregiver's crown on her head and let her reign as queen for the day—or forever.

In 2 Timothy 4:7-8, Paul wrote, "I have kept the faith. Now, a crown is being held for me—a crown for being right with God."

Mom isn't a saint because she takes care of Grandma's physical needs or because she prays for her and with her. And maybe her diligence isn't something that will inspire an hour-long Oprah show. The truth is, her life lived before others has taught "Jesus love" to many, whether she ever wears a crown in this life or not.

Does Mom think she needs a crown? Maybe some days when grandma is difficult, but usually they're having too much fun to think about other rewards. ⇒

ACTION STEP

HOW DO YOU HONOR YOUR PARENTS? A GIFT ON MOTHER'S AND FATHER'S DAY AND AN OCCASIONAL PHONE CALL? THINK OF FIVE SPECIAL WAYS TO SHOW RESPECT AND LOVE FOR YOUR PARENTS, THINGS THAT WILL MAKE THEM FEEL HONORED AND APPRECIATED. AS YOU PUT THEM INTO PRACTICE, BE BLESSED KNOWING YOU'LL MAKE THEIR DAY—AND YOURS!

PRAYER

Father, please give me a heart ready to care for others. Please use me to bless my family today.

TEACHING FAITH

THE MOST IMPORTANT TASK FOR A MOTHER IS TO TEACH HER CHILDREN LOVE FOR AND FAITH IN GOD.

Faith is not taught as much as it's caught.

ANONYMOUS

TO THINK ABOUT

- ⚷ Who helped you to believe in God and learn to love Him?
- ⚷ What were some of the ways they passed on faith in God?
- ⚷ What can you do to help your children fall in love with Jesus?

LESSON FOR LIFE

Promises

God will:

Make you a light
in your world
Matthew 5:14

Bless your children and
their children through
your faithfulness
Deuteronomy 11:21

Give you wisdom
Exodus 4:15

Passing the Torch

BIBLE STUDY PASSAGE: DEUTERONOMY 11:1-21

*Obey his laws and commands that I am giving you today
so that things will go well for you and your children. Then
you will live a long time in the land that the Lord your
God is giving to you forever.*

DEUTERONOMY 4:40

It has been said that faith in God is always one generation
from extinction. That's why it's so important for parents to pass
on the faith they have received from others.

Some of the most important ways you can build in your
children a sense of faith in God are—

- Talk about God in your home. In a less hectic age, family
devotion time was more the norm than the exception it
is today. In the mad dash of activities, find time each
day to read God's Word and pray with your children. And
make talk of Jesus a natural, normal part of conversation.
"Teach them [God's commandments] well to your
children, talking about them when you sit at home and

walk along the road, when you lie down and when you get up" (Deuteronomy 11:19).

- Take your kids to church—and attend as well. The writer of Hebrews reminds his readers: "You should not stay away from the church meetings, as some are doing, but you should meet together and encourage each other" (Hebrews 10:24). Faith is not something that is practiced in isolation, but always thrives best in a family and community setting. So don't just drop kids off for Sunday school—let them see you there. Get to know other families with like faith and values.
- Model faith for them. Since faith is caught more than taught, they need to see it lived out by their mom. Pray. Be positive. Ask for forgiveness. Grant forgiveness. Be kind. In other words, ask the Holy Spirit to help you live the "fruit of the Spirit" in front of your children: "But the Spirit produces the fruit of love, joy, peace, patience, kindness, goodness, faithfulness, gentleness, self-control" (Galatians 5:22-23).
- Pray for your child. You need the help of the Church, but you also need the help of the Holy Spirit. Pray for your children's faith every day, because as Jesus says, "If you ask me for anything in my name, I will do it" (John 14:14). ➔

Children, come and listen to me. I will teach you to worship the Lord.
Proverbs 34:11

REAL LIFE

The Prayer of a Mother

C. HOPE FLINCHBAUGH

Corrie Ten Boom often spoke warmly of her growing up years in Haarlem, Holland. She recalled a home full of food, compassion, and people hard on their luck looking for help.

She remembered her mother's love—the kind lady took baskets of food to the poor and the sick, helped her husband in his watch shop, and even cared for their extended family. A devoted mother, she nurtured Corrie and her sisters and brother, teaching them to love God and love people with all their hearts and resources. She made prayer, scripture study, and service a regular and foremost part of their daily rituals.

Corrie looks back especially fondly on a day when she was about five years old. She was playing with her doll, Casperina, in the kitchen, and turned a kitchen chair around backwards to pretend it was the door of her neighbor's house.

Corrie carried Casperina around the edge of the kitchen, imagining she was skipping along the road to the neighbor's house. She stopped at the chair and knocked on it, then waited for the imaginary occupant to answer. No one came.

She knocked again. *Knock, knock, knock.*

"Corrie," her mother gently interrupted. "I know someone who is standing at your door and knocking right now."

Corrie looked around the kitchen. "What door, Mama?"

"Your door, Corrie," Mama answered. "Jesus said He is standing at the door of your heart, and if you invite Him in, He will come into your heart. Would you like to invite Him in?"

Corrie thought about it for a moment. Then she answered, "Yes, Mama. I want Jesus in my heart."

When she finished praying to receive Jesus, she looked up into her mother's face. She had never seen her mama look so radiantly beautiful. The whole kitchen looked beautiful—the ivory walls were suddenly more soothing, the drapes suddenly more cheerful.

As Corrie grew up, she began to follow her parents' example in taking care of those in need around her. Sadly, her mother grew very ill as she got older, becoming paralyzed and unable to speak. When she died, Corrie and her sister Betsy carried the torch of their mother's service in the neighborhood, taking in foster children and working with the mentally handicapped.

When the Second World War began to brew, Corrie's heart was wrenched by the desperation and destitution growing around her, and she felt God giving her an even greater love and compassion for others. So she began to devote much of her time to helping her family hide and care for Jews and members of the Dutch underground who were being hunted by the Nazis.

After surviving a concentration camp, she wrote classic thoughts on forgiveness and hope, such as: "There is no pit so deep that God's love is not deeper still." She has become an icon of Christian faith, service, love, and self-sacrifice—all because her mother knelt on a kitchen floor and prayed on a very ordinary afternoon. ➤

ACTION STEP

WHEN IT COMES TO FOSTERING YOUR CHILDREN'S FAITH IN AND DEVOTION TO GOD, THE BEST PLACE TO START IS WITH YOURSELF. IF YOU'RE NOT REGULARLY SPENDING TIME IN DEVOTIONS, NOW'S THE TIME TO START. THERE ARE LOTS OF SCRIPTURE-READING PLANS TO BE FOUND ONLINE AND IN DEVOTIONAL BOOKS AND BIBLES. ONCE YOU HAVE A HABIT IN PLACE, IT MIGHT BE TIME TO VISIT A BOOKSTORE AND PICK OUT AGE-APPROPRIATE DEVOTION BOOKS FOR YOUR WHOLE FAMILY.

PRAYER

Lord, I know that nothing is more important than teaching my kids to follow You—and that there's no better way to do that than to follow You myself. Please give me a contagious love for You, Lord God.

LOSING A CHILD

GOD IS KIND AND GENTLE AS HE HEALS A BROKEN HEART.

God is closest to those with broken hearts.

JEWISH SAYING

TO THINK ABOUT

- How have you handled losses in your life?
- What things in your life do you hold most dear?
- What are ways that knowing God provides spiritual resources for the ups and downs of life?

LESSON FOR LIFE

Promises

God Will:

Put an end to suffering

Revelation 21:4

Heal the grieving

Psalm 147:3

Comfort you

Psalm 94:19

Use you to

comfort others

2 Corinthians 1:4

Wounded Healers

BIBLE STUDY PASSAGE: 1 CORINTHIANS 1:26-2:4

He comforts us every time we have trouble, so when others have trouble, we can comfort them with the same comfort God gives us.

2 CORINTHIANS 1:4

How could such a promising future go wrong so fast? All of us have witnessed instances when a friend or loved one has experienced devastating pain—divorce, depression, alcoholism, the death of a child, a traumatic accident, a devastating illness.

The message of 2 Corinthians 1:3-6 is that there is hope for the broken. No life is filled with so much pain that the God of all comfort cannot reach down with a healing touch. Whether you are in need of a personal touch from God in your own life or are walking beside someone else who is broken, some words of encouragement include—

- God never forsakes us (Hebrews 13:5): God is kind and merciful, and always on our side. He is present in the midst of all circumstances.

- God can turn tragedy into triumph (Psalm 30:11): Even in the darkest moments of the soul, God provides a supernatural comfort and perspective that allows individuals to experience and exhibit God's love and power.
- God sends helpers (Galatians 6:10): Even though God is all-powerful and can intervene directly in healing, more often He sends human helpers, including doctors and counselors, to work on His behalf. It is no lack of faith to turn to others for help.
- God heals all infirmities in eternity (1 Corinthians 15:42-43): Yes, God miraculously heals people today—but not in all cases. Paul gives the eternal perspective when he reminds us: "The sufferings we have now are nothing compared to the great glory that will be shown to us" (Romans 8:18).

No human words or thoughts can explain away or provide comfort for certain kinds of suffering and pain. Maybe God doesn't want us to be able to do so. But His ultimate expression of comfort is the gift of salvation and eternal life through the death of His Son Jesus Christ (1 Peter 3:18). ➡

When he came near the town gate, he saw a funeral. A mother, who was a widow, had lost her only son. A large crowd from the town was with the mother while her son was being carried out. When the Lord saw her, he felt very sorry for her and said, "Don't cry."
Luke 7:12-13

REAL LIFE

From Mourning to Morning

LOUISE TUCKER JONES

It had been several sad and lonely weeks since my three-month-old son, Travis, had died suddenly with congenital heart disease. In fact, the weeks had now turned into months, and whereas I held onto God with all my strength soon after his death, I now wanted nothing to do with Him. I was so angry at God for taking my son that I vowed to never pray to Him again.

There was just one problem: my four-year-old son, Aaron. He missed his brother dearly and every day he would ask me questions like "Mommy, what's heaven like?" "Mommy, can I go to heaven and see Travis?" Or, "Mommy, why can't Daddy go get Travis and bring him home?" These are tough questions, especially when you are mad at God.

I couldn't stand the thought of hurting Aaron with the bitterness that was consuming me. I had taught him every day of his young life that Jesus loved him. I could not bear to destroy that faith. I knew I had to find peace beyond my grief so that I could be a good mother to Aaron.

Finally, one night, as I lay alone on my bed in the darkened room, I poured out my heart to God—my anger, bitterness, and pain. I prayed, "Lord, I have tried to change, but I can't; so if You want me whole again, You will have to do it."

Suddenly, the room was filled with an almost palatable peace and I heard God speak to my heart, "Louise, Travis is with Me." Then, to my amazement, I felt the weight of my baby son placed against by breast and could almost feel his hair brush against my cheek. I couldn't open my eyes as tears streamed across my temples, soaking my hair. I lay absolutely still, allowing God to comfort me in a way I had never known as I continued listening to His gentle whisper, "Travis is okay. He's with Me."

When I awoke the next morning, the bitterness and anger were gone. I still missed my son terribly. I still had no explanation for the deep *why* in my heart. But I had the most intimate encounter with God's love and presence that I had ever experienced in my entire life. ⇒

ACTION STEP

IN GENESIS 22:1-14, WE READ THE POIGNANT STORY OF HOW ABRAHAM WAS WILLING TO SACRIFICE BACK TO GOD WHAT HE MOST CHERISHED. HIS LOVE FOR GOD WAS THAT GREAT. AND GOD'S LOVE FOR ABRAHAM WAS SUCH THAT HE GAVE BACK TO ABRAHAM HIS HEART'S DESIRE. WHAT DO YOU DESIRE MOST IN LIFE? HAVE YOU EVER EXPRESSED TO GOD THAT YOU LOVE HIM SO MUCH THAT HE COMES BEFORE ALL ELSE? FIND A WAY TO EXPRESS THAT TODAY. IF THE FEELINGS AREN'T THERE—IF YOU'RE HAVING TROUBLE HONESTLY SAYING TO GOD THAT YOU WOULD LOVE HIM EVEN IF THE MOST PRECIOUS THING IN YOUR LIFE WAS TAKEN AWAY—EXPRESS TO GOD THAT YOU WANT TO REACH THAT LEVEL OF LOVE FOR AND TRUST IN HIM.

PRAYER

Father, thank You for healing us and redeeming us. Thank You for strength in the midst of anguish. Help me cling to Your love and power today. Amen.

LETTING GO

AFTER YEARS OF GUIDING AND
CORRECTING, THERE COMES A TIME
WHEN ALL WE CAN DO IS LOVE OUR KIDS
AND ENTRUST THEM TO GOD'S HANDS.

*The greatest gifts you can give your children are the
roots of responsibility and the wings of independence.*

DENIS WAITLEY

To Think About

- Do you think today's youth are equipped to make good decisions?
- Do you ever find yourself taking over responsibilities that your kids should take on themselves?
- What are you doing to help your children make a lifetime of wise and godly choices?

LESSON FOR LIFE

Promises

God Will:

Help your kids thrive

Psalm 102:28

Guide your kids'
steps—and yours!
Isaiah 30:21
Proverbs 3:5-6

Give you peace
as you trust Him
Isaiah 26:3

The Loving Father

BIBLE STUDY PASSAGE: LUKE 15

While the son was still a long way off, his father saw him
and felt sorry for his son. So the father ran to him and
hugged and kissed him.

LUKE 15:20

Jesus used parables to teach a single, major truth He
wanted His listeners to understand. That's why it may be more
accurate to title the parable of the "Prodigal Son" the parable of
the "Loving Father." Jesus teaches us that God's love extends
not just to those who "stay home" and obey, but even to those
who rebel and squander their spiritual inheritance.

But this parable also contains some subpoints that teach
valuable lessons about ourselves, including a few hard-hitting
lessons for parents—

- You can raise kids in a godly home and they still might
  choose to be disobedient. In the Old Testament, Ezekiel
  taught that the son won't be blamed for his father's sins,
  but the father won't be blamed for the son's sins either:

"A child will not be punished for a parent's sin, and a parent will not be punished for a child's sin" (Ezekiel 18:20).

- It is right to let kids make their own choices over time. Is there one exact way to do this? Probably not. But a good rule of thumb would be that the elementary years are for "forming" and the teen years are for "letting go." That obviously doesn't mean withdrawing rules and guidance at age thirteen. It must be a slow progression.
- Even if our kids hurt and disappoint us with their decisions, we should never give up on them or try to take control of their lives. They will always need our love— and that love is what God may use to guide them.

The bottom line is that all parents, whether their kids are living wisely or foolishly at any given moment, must trust them into God's hands and grace. ➔

I prayed for this child, and the Lord answered my prayer and gave him to me. Now I give him back to the Lord. He will belong to the Lord all his life.
1 Samuel 1:27-28

REAL LIFE

Giving My Daughter Wings

MARCIA LEE LAYCOCK

I could feel the pull in my daughter's voice during the long-distance call. She wanted me to tell her what she should do. Our middle daughter, Laura was in between in more ways than one. Having graduated from college, she had been working, but was restless. She felt the Lord had something more for her.

So she took a leap of faith and applied to do mission work in Asia. As she launched herself onto this path, she had to make some big decisions—something that has never been easy for Laura. A perpetually positive person, she saw good in every option and had a hard time deciding which was best.

A struggle between options was what had led her to call me that afternoon. Should she stay in the city, where she was paying high rent and driving a fair distance to a job that was not very challenging? Or should she come home? She'd be able to save more money living with us and could work for a friend to pay off her student loan more quickly, but that would mean leaving a good group of friends and a good church in which she was active. She just couldn't decide.

As a mom, my first instinct was to tell her what to do. In fact, I wanted to shout—"Come home!" But I restrained myself and told her I would keep praying for God's direction.

The next morning, I was reading my Bible and came across Psalm 84. Verse 3 seemed to flash like a neon sign: "The sparrows have found a home, and the swallows have nests. They raise their young near your altars, Lord All-Powerful, my King and my God."

I e-mailed the verse to Laura and told her, "Nest yourself near the Lord, and it won't matter where you fly."

I asked God to help her make the best decision for her life. I desperately prayed that she would nest in Him, come close to Him. But I couldn't do it for her.

When Laura did come home, I realized it wasn't going be easy to watch her face the challenges and struggles of life. It wouldn't be easy to deal with my fears for her safety. I had to bite my tongue several times, not wanting my words of worry to squelch her assurance of God's call.

But as I have prayed for her, facing and confessing my fears, I have realized I have decisions to make, too, decisions regarding faith, decisions regarding trust. As Laura takes flight under God's wings, I have some nesting of my own to do.

I've realized that when I heed God's gentle whisper, "Abide in Me. Hide in Me. Let Me gather you under My wing. Stay close," I find peace. When I trust Him, I am strong enough to give my daughter the encouragement she needs to chart her course and soar. ➔

ACTION STEP

ONE OF THE REASONS THAT HOBBIES ARE SO IMPORTANT FOR CHILDREN IS THAT IT GIVES THEM A GREAT OPPORTUNITY TO TAKE PERSONAL RESPONSIBILITY FOR A TASK. IN TODAY'S TV-SATURATED CULTURE, MANY KIDS DON'T MAKE MODELS, COLLECT STAMPS, GROW GARDENS, OR OTHER HEALTHY ACTIVITIES.

NO MATTER WHAT YOUR CHILDREN'S AGES, MAYBE YOU CAN TAKE THEM OUT TO LOOK FOR AN APPROPRIATE HOBBY. WHETHER IT'S SOMETHING ATHLETIC LIKE RUNNING WITH A RUNNING CLUB, SOMETHING STUDIOUS LIKE COLLECTING COINS, OR SOMETHING ARTISTIC LIKE PAINTING OR SCULPTING, WHO KNOWS BETTER THAN YOU WHAT CAPTURES THEIR INTERESTS? ASK THEM WHAT THEY'D MOST LIKE TO DO, AND HELP THEM GET ON THEIR WAY TODAY!

PRAYER

Lord, I know You love my children even more than I do. I pray that You would draw close to me and to them today and help us to trust You.

HEAVEN

GOD'S GIFT OF SALVATION MEANS THAT WE WILL LIVE FOREVER IN GLORY.

To go to heaven, fully to enjoy God, is infinitely better than the most pleasant accommodations here.

JONATHAN EDWARDS

TO THINK ABOUT

- ☞ Why is heaven so hard to describe?
- ☞ What are some of the images that flash in your mind when you think of heaven?
- ☞ What do you think is important for kids to understand about heaven?

LESSON FOR LIFE

Promises

God will:

Prepare something
wonderful for those
who love Him
1 Corinthians 2:9

Save those who
believe in Him
John 3:16

Heal in heaven
Revelation 21:4

Prepare a place without
pain or darkness
Revelation 22:5

The Glory of Heaven

BIBLE STUDY PASSAGE: JOHN 14:1-27

There are many rooms in my Father's house; I would not tell you this if it were not true. I am going there to prepare a place for you.

JOHN 14:2

While it's true that our focus needs to be on serving God and others today (Matthew 6:33); and while it's also true that we can experience the full riches of heaven right now (Ephesians 2:6); it is also true that we receive comfort and encouragement as we think about our future in heaven.

Heaven truly is a wonderful place!

- It's a place of beauty: "No one has ever imagined what God has prepared for those who love him" (1 Corinthians 2:9). No words can adequately describe the wonder of heaven.
- It's a place of restoration: "He will wipe away every tear from their eyes, and there will be no more death, sadness, crying, or pain" (Revelation 21:4). All sorrows and infirmities disappear and are healed in heaven.

- It's a place of divine presence: "Now God's presence is with people, and he will live with them, and they will be his people" (Revelation 21:3). We know Jesus and love Jesus right now. But think how wonderful it will be to see Him face-to-face.
- It's a place of purity: "There will never be night again. They will not need the light of a lamp or the light of the sun, because the Lord God will give them light" (Revelation 22:5). Sin and anything that distorts the true pleasures and fulfillment of humanity will no longer corrupt.
- It's a place of joy "Because you were loyal with small things, I will let you care for much greater things. Come and share my joy with me" (Matthew 25:21). Think of the happiest day you have ever experienced. It will not compare to the joy you will celebrate in heaven.

A final benefit of thinking about heaven is that it motivates us to serve God joyfully now—and reach out to children, our spouse, other family members, friends, and even enemies with the love of God today. ➤

We know that our body—the tent we live in here on earth—will be destroyed. But when that happens, God will have a house for us. It will not be a house made by human hands; instead, it will be a home in heaven that will last forever.

2 Corinthians 5:1

REAL LIFE

Lesson from a Fish

TONYA RUIZ

Waking to a loud noise, I sleepily headed towards the light in the kitchen. *Who is up?* I wondered.

Three-year-old Ashley had scooted a chair over to the counter. Her bobbed haircut covered her face as she looked down into the goldfish bowl. The coveted prize from the fair, Sammy the goldfish, was floating on his side.

"I think you fed him too much, honey," I told her.

"But he always looked hungry—he kept going like this," she replied, dramatically reenacting Sammy's familiar opening and closing of his mouth while flapping her bent arms like fins. Considering the seriousness of the moment, I tried not to smile at her adorable goldfish impersonation.

"Why isn't he swimming around in circles, Mommy?"

"He's dead, honey."

"What's dead?"

"That means he won't swim or eat anymore. He's not alive."

"Poor Sammy," she said, her voice choked with emotion.

Oh, sweetie, life is already hard. I'm sorry.

"It's too early for you to be up." I said, "I'll tuck you back into bed."

I kissed her sad angel face, pulled the covers over her pink-ruffled Barbie pajamas, and turned her light out.

I went into the bathroom and unceremoniously dumped Sammy from his glass bowl into the toilet bowl and flushed. Then I flushed again. He finally went down. The third time's a charm.

Later, at the breakfast table, Ashley held the now-obsolete little pink castle from the goldfish bowl. Salty tears ran down her cheeks and mixed with the milk in her cereal bowl.

"What will happen when I die, Mommy?" she asked, her sweet little button-nosed face looking so serious.

I paused a moment, caught off-guard by the question. Then I answered, "You'll go to heaven and live with Jesus forever."

"What's heaven like?"

"The Bible says it's beautiful. The streets are made of shiny gold."

I went to the bookshelf, brought back a children's story about heaven, and we went into the living room and snuggled up on the couch.

"In heaven there will be no more tears..." the book began.

"Will there be candy?" she asked, still sniffling.

"I suppose so," I said. "Everyone is happy in heaven."

Ashley jumped off my lap and ran to her bedroom. I heard her closet door open and sounds of frantic searching. She came back carrying her favorite sandals and struggled to put them on. I sat wondering, *What is she up to?*

She looked up at me and impatiently said, "Quick, Mom, get your shoes. Let's go."

"Where are we going?" ➡

"I wanna go to heaven."

"Soon enough, Ashley, soon enough."

"We can't go now?"

"No, honey, not today."

"Can I get a new goldfish?"

"That we can do."

I slipped on my shoes and grabbed my car key. Then we drove to the pet store to buy Sammy #2.

ACTION STEP

WHO WILL BE IN HEAVEN BECAUSE OF YOU? THE SONG BY RAY BOLTZ SAYS, "THANK YOU FOR GIVING TO THE LORD. I AM A LIFE THAT WAS CHANGED."

WRITE DOWN FIVE NAMES OF THOSE WHO NEED TO KNOW GOD. BEGIN PRAYING FOR THEIR SOULS TODAY. ASK GOD TO HELP YOU REACH OUT TO THEM AT THE RIGHT TIME IN THE RIGHT PLACE.

PRAYER

Father God, thank You so much that You have provided a place without pain and a way to get there. Please help me today to reflect the glory of heaven in my life right now.

KIDS-IN-LAW

OUR RELATIONSHIP WITH OUR KID'S SPOUSE CAN SUPPORT OR DAMAGE THEIR MARRIAGE AND OUR FUTURE RELATIONSHIP.

The young man who wasn't good enough for
our daughter always turns out to be the father
of the smartest grandchildren in the world.

ANONYMOUS

 TO THINK ABOUT

- Does the thought of your child getting married one day fill you with joy or apprehension—or both?
- How much guidance should a parent offer on the choice of their child's mate? What if a parent sees them making what they believe to be a mistake?
- How can loving your child's spouse help their marriage grow?

LESSON FOR LIFE

Promises

God Will:

See that love prevails
1 Peter 4:8

Forgive you as you
forgive others
Matthew 6:14-15

Continue to work in
your children's lives
Romans 8:28

Mother of the Bride (or Groom)

BIBLE STUDY PASSAGE: RUTH 1:6-18

It takes wisdom to have a good family, and it takes understanding to make it strong.

PROVERBS 24:3

In teaching His disciples about the power of persistent prayer, Jesus said to them, "Even though you are bad, you know how to give good gifts to your children. How much more your heavenly Father will give good things to those who ask him!" (Matthew 7:11).

His point was the perfect goodness of our Heavenly Father, but He also reminds us that good parents want good things for their kids—including a great spouse one day.

Our healthy desire for their best is a blessing to our kids as it shows them how much we care and helps lift their expectations higher, but occasionally it can be a negative dynamic when we are harsh toward a future spouse (or current spouse) because not all of our expectations are met.

Consider a few proactive measures—or if your child is already married, a few reactive measures might be in order.

- Work on your own marriage. Model for your children affection, forgiveness, kindness, grace, and enjoyment. If you are single, carefully watch what you say about your exspouse and model quiet dignity along with the other traits listed above.
- Pray with your children, and frequently include a prayer of blessing for their futures—and their future spouses.
- Be involved with your children's friends. Since peer relationships are a huge determinant in your children's lifestyle as they move through their teen years and into adulthood, stay close to the situation. Hold as many activities as you can at your house. Talk to their friends—including anyone they date.
- When your children marry, add to their "attractiveness" by creating a fun, friendly family support network that the spouses enjoy. Some young men or women have fallen in love with a family before falling in love with the person they marry. Do your best to build these dynamics before and after the weddings. It might help them navigate the inevitable rough waters all couples experience.

Remember, one of the best ways you will express love to your adult children is in how you express love to their spouses. ➡

> Get along with each other, and forgive each other. If someone does wrong to you, forgive that person because the Lord forgave you.
>
> Colossians 3:13

 REAL LIFE

Rooting Out the Problem

JOANNE SCHULTE

Outwardly it appeared everything was good between us, but inwardly I was disappointed with my daughter's husband. He seemed like a nice guy and they were happy together, but I couldn't help but focus on the things he lacked—those qualities I wished he had. And so, growing in the garden of my heart was what the Bible refers to as a "root of bitterness."

Since they lived some distance away, it was easy to pretend the problem didn't exist, to ignore it and hope it would go away. I didn't want them to see the bitterness I felt towards their marriage.

One Sunday, I attended church with them, and the pastor preached on removing a root of bitterness (referring to Hebrews 12:14-15). He emphasized how destructive bitterness can be, and stressed the importance of dealing with it right away lest it damage a relationship.

I certainly didn't want that.

He was right, of course, and now that I had been reminded of this truth, it was my responsibility to deal with it. It was uncomfortable to hear the potential consequences of my bitterness, but his words were just the encouragement I needed to make me do something about it. But what should I do?

As I went about my daily chores the next week, the pastor's words played over and over again in my thoughts—"damage a relationship," and I prayed to the Master Gardener to show me how to remove the root of bitterness. All I could think about was that I had to get rid of the root before it sprouted and hurt someone.

After I prayed, conviction pierced my heart. I got out my stationery and wrote a note through tear-filled eyes to my daughter and son-in-law confessing my attitude and asking for their forgiveness.

It wasn't an easy letter to write. I wasn't sure if my son-in-law would be crushed and hate me forever, if my daughter would want to have a long discussion and dissect in detail exactly what I didn't like about her husband, or just how this letter would impact our future relationship. But as I dropped it in the mailbox, I knew a heavy load had been lifted from my heart.

To my relief and delight, their prompt reply was loving, gracious, and forgiving, and they were not even aware I had harbored any bitterness. Even better, the Master Gardener did a thorough job of removing the roots of bitterness from my heart in the weeks that followed.

Recently, our whole family got together, and when pictures were being taken, my son-in-law put his arm around me and said, "Get my picture with Mom." I hugged his shoulder as we cheesed for the camera. We have a good relationship—comfortable, fun, loving, and completely free of bitterness.

I will always be thankful to the Master Gardener for restoring my relationship with my daughter and son-in-law. ➻

ACTION STEP

THE NEXT TIME YOU PRAY WITH YOUR CHILDREN, TEACH THEM TO PRAY FOR
THEIR FUTURE SPOUSES. ASK GOD FOR PROTECTION AND BLESSINGS FOR
BOTH YOUR CHILDREN AND THE PERSON THEY MARRY. ASK HIM TO HELP
THEM KNOW WHAT TO DO AND TO GIVE THEM GOOD CHARACTER. AND THANK
HIM FOR HIS GOOD GIFTS!

PRAYER

*Father God, I know someday it will be time to welcome a new member of my
family. I just ask You to send my kids someone great. Please guide my children's spouses safely to them and bless their lives together.*

INTERCESSORY PRAYER

WE ARE CALLED TO EXTEND OUR FAITH AND PRAYERS ON BEHALF OF OTHERS.

*We must move from asking God to take care of
the things that are breaking our hearts, to praying
about the things that are breaking His heart.*

MARGARET GIBB

To Think About

- Have you ever sensed that someone is praying for you? Do you know someone who is praying for you?
- Who are you praying for right now?
- Do you believe that your faith and prayers can make a difference in someone else's life?

LESSON FOR LIFE

Promises

The Intercessor

BIBLE STUDY PASSAGE: ROMANS 8:26-34

God will:

By helping each other with your troubles, you truly obey
Hear your prayers *the law of Christ.*

John 14:14

GALATIANS 6:2

1 Peter 3:12

Reward persistence
and prayer

Matthew 7:7

Build up His people

Deuteronomy 28:9

Be among those
gathered in His name

Matthew 18:20

James, the head of the early church in Jerusalem, said that
if anyone is sick, call for the elders of the church to lay hands on
that person and anoint them with oil for their healing (5:14).
Paul challenges the church in Galatians to "restore" to salvation the person who has fallen away from their Christian walk
(6:15). Jesus sent all His disciples into the world to make new
disciples in His name (Matthew 28:19-20). Throughout the
Bible, we read that we really do need each other. Faith is not a
solitary journey. The Church works like a body and each part is
needed for it to work right (1 Corinthians 12:13-18).

One of the most dynamic expressions of this interrelated-
ness is intercessory prayer. This is when we add our faith on
top of or in place of another person's faith. Maybe they have
fallen into a pit of despair or a trap of sin and their faith is weak
or nonexistent. Maybe they are too young to be totally

accountable or aware of an issue like illness or trauma in their
life. Whatever the case, one of the greatest ways we can
express love and support to someone is when we ask God to act
on their behalf—for healing, forgiveness, reconciliation, peace,
and a myriad of other issues. Amazingly, God will honor our
faith through the Holy Spirit and impress our prayers on that
person's heart.

When a believing person prays, great things happen.
James 5:16

Another incredible promise and source of comfort that we
can cling to is that the Holy Spirit prays on our behalf, beyond
our own understanding of our needs (Romans 8:26-27), and
Jesus is our intercessor who constantly speaks to God the
Father on our behalf (Hebrews 7:25).

Whatever your need—or the need of your loved one—be
assured that your faith united with the faith of others creates
miracles! ➡

REAL LIFE

My Tiny Wooden Cup

GLENDA PALMER

A tiny wooden communion cup—a special gift—sits on my nightstand, and each night when I go to bed, it reminds me of God's presence. Our twenty-three-year-old son had just undergone surgery. The medical diagnosis: cancer—and the doctors didn't get it all.

Within a few days, his room was crowded with flowers and cards and caring, praying friends. My prayer partner sent a "heal"ium balloon to him.

What an encouragement my prayer partner was! She gave me some powerful scriptures which spoke to me of the all-sufficiency of Christ. She also gave me the little wooden communion cup with this note from another friend attached: "In Christ your child is my child and I shall shelter him in prayer as if he were my own. We are joining in communion for him each evening. The wee cup is your symbol of the covenant. You know of my love for you. Call anytime. I will not call you at present, but I will call to God who gives wisdom."

A few days later, several people gathered in our living room to anoint our son with oil and pray for his healing. My tiny wooden cup held the olive oil we used.

I wrote in my journal when I was in the middle of the fire:

We have joined the fellowship of Christ's suffering. With so many of His children crying out, "Abba, Father," on behalf of our son, I know He hears us and I know

He is able. Our son is God's child and I am God's child, too. Our cups are empty but He is able to fill them. He alone is able. To Him be the glory.

Now, fifteen years later, I look back on my son's illness, one of those "impossible situations" that come into our lives, I can still feel the pain I felt—but I also still feel the amazing grace and love that the family of God poured out on us during that time.

Each morning, I prayed and studied my Bible. Those words were my marching orders for the day. Hymns and praise songs were God speaking to me and me to Him. The Lord sent other people who were His angels to minister to me and pray without ceasing for Kent. God's grace! Yes! It was sufficient! It really was, whatever the outcome.

That was one of the hardest lessons that God wanted to teach me—"whatever the outcome." I needed to trust Jesus and love Him even if He chose to take our son to heaven. It took time to come to that place, but it was a place of peace. I wouldn't have come to that place without the diligent prayers of my brothers and sisters in Christ.

God answered our prayers with a yes. Our son is alive and well, married to a precious Christian wife, and father to our thirteen-year-old granddaughter. To Him is all the glory! →

ACTION STEP

DO YOU HAVE A SPECIAL NEED IN YOUR LIFE RIGHT NOW? A HUGE DECISION? A PHYSICAL AILMENT? A MONEY ISSUE? PROBLEMS WITH YOUR CHILD OR SPOUSE OR A CLOSE FRIEND? GATHER A SMALL TRUSTED GROUP OF FRIENDS TO PRAY WITH YOU. PROVIDE THEM WITH SPECIFIC WAYS THAT THEY CAN AGREE WITH YOU IN PRAYER.

PRAYER

Thank You that even now the Holy Spirit is expressing to You the needs of my heart and life. Thank You that Jesus Christ has interceded with You for the forgiveness of my sins.

WILLING HEARTS

GOD DOES NOT USUALLY SHOUT NOR FORCE US TO LISTEN, SO WE MUST MAINTAIN OPEN AND RECEPTIVE HEARTS.

God delights in seeing us share our time, money,
and resources for no reason other than the joy
of giving. When our motives are pure, then
giving is not only easy, it's downright fun.

LIZ CURTIS HIGGS

 TO THINK ABOUT

- Do you believe that God speaks directly to people today?
- Have you ever sensed God's voice in your life?
- If God wanted to get hold of you with a special task, how hard would it be to get your attention?

LESSON FOR LIFE

Promises

God will:

Speak to you

1 Kings 19:12

Reveal His will

Psalm 32:8

Increase your faith

2 Thessalonians 1:3

Hear your prayers

Psalm 116:1

A Whisper in the Night

BIBLE STUDY PASSAGE: 1 SAMUEL 3:10

Speak, Lord. I am your servant and I am listening.

1 SAMUEL 3:10

Sometimes we panic about what we're supposed to do. Which doctor? Which school? Which neighborhood? In our frenzy to do the right thing, how attentively do we listen for God's voice to lead and direct us?

God speaks to everyone through His Word. Everything we need to know about loving Him and others is clearly spelled out. But sometimes God speaks in special ways, under special circumstances, with a special message to us individually.

God speaks to us through—

- Our own thoughts—if we read His Word and talk to Him in prayer, it shouldn't surprise us when we begin coming up with ideas that seem heaven-sent. "Pray to me, and I will answer you. I will tell you important secrets you have never heard before" (Jeremiah 33:3).
- The thoughts of others—again, if we talk about God with others who know Him and love Him, we should expect to

hear His voice in the words of a trusted friend. "A good person speaks with wisdom, and he says what is fair" (Psalm 37:30).

- A question or problem that won't go away—often, when we sense a special need in our community or in our own life, God is prompting us to discover something He wants us to do about it through us. God gave Paul a mission to Macedonia through a vision of a Macedonian man begging for help (see Acts 16:9-10).

- A sermon or song—when we go to church with an open heart and mind, we should expect to hear a special word from God through the music and preaching. "Come, let us go up to the mountain of the Lord, to the Temple of the God of Jacob. Then God will teach us his ways, and we will obey his teachings" (Isaiah 2:3).

- A still, small voice—though people might think we're crazy, it's true that God does directly impress His thoughts on our minds today. Even as He called Samuel to be His prophet in the still of the night (1 Samuel 3:4), sometimes He chooses to make Himself known directly on our hearts.

The real question is not whether God speaks today, but how well do we listen? ➢

My sheep listen to my voice; I know them, and they follow me.
John 10:27

 ## REAL LIFE

Postal Prayer

CAROL LOY

"I can't have a life with these kids around," my daughter raged. "I can't get a job or go to school because I can't afford child care, and I never get to go out with my friends. I can't even take my eyes off them for a second!"

"That's what toddlers do, they get into things. That's how they learn," I offered quietly, not pressing the issue too hard because we had disagreed too often about her other complaints. Each time she had a new baby by the latest great love in her life, I had begged her to think about her children, but she was still looking for Mr. Right in every bar in town.

I hoped this was just a fleeting tantrum. But my heart ached as I realized she was completing a pattern started eight months earlier when she talked us into taking her four- and five-year-old sons (just temporarily). How could this woman we had adopted when she was ten—because we had wanted children— say this about her remaining two children, a three-year-old son and a fifteen-month-old daughter?

As I cradled the children in my arms and cried inside, I knew what I had to do. I could not force her to keep these two precious children she didn't want.

I delayed taking them home, giving myself one night to talk to my husband. He had a little fit of his own: *No way! You're out of your mind! We're too old to start over. Our house is too small. We've raised our family.*

They moved in the next day. One night, he was walking the floor with a screaming baby when she opened her eyes, saw who held her, and smiled as she wrapped her arms around his neck. He hasn't told me I'm out of my mind since.

We're building a five-room addition to our home, though it's going slowly as my husband left his contracting job for one with a steady income and health insurance. As for myself, I now stay at home with the children and take on freelance writing projects.

When the baby, starved for affection, unplugs my computer to get my attention, I silently echo my daughter's complaints. Life isn't as easy with kids around—especially at my age—but the difference is that my husband and I want these children. We want to love them and bring them up to have good lives, knowing God is there for them. Bottom line, we are both convinced that God spoke to us and told us to raise these kids—and that anytime you say yes to God, your life is blessed.

One evening, we were relaxing after tucking all four little ones into bed. I was reading a story in the newspaper about a letter delivered by the postal service twenty years after it was mailed, when my husband asked if I remembered how hard we had prayed for babies twenty years earlier.

I burst into laughter. After I read him the article, he laughed too. "So that's how we did it. We routed our prayers through the postal service and God's answer came—in His own good time." ➡

ACTION STEP

JAMES SAYS OF WISDOM THAT "IF ANY OF YOU NEEDS WISDOM, YOU SHOULD ASK GOD FOR IT. HE IS GENEROUS AND ENJOYS GIVING TO ALL PEOPLE, SO HE WILL GIVE YOU WISDOM. BUT WHEN YOU ASK GOD, YOU MUST BELIEVE AND NOT DOUBT. ANYONE WHO DOUBTS IS LIKE A WAVE IN THE SEA, BLOWN UP AND DOWN BY THE WIND" (1:5-6). WHEN WAS THE LAST TIME YOU SPECIFICALLY ASKED GOD TO SPEAK TO YOU ABOUT A PARTICULAR STRUGGLE? A RELATIONSHIP ISSUE? YOUR FUTURE? YOUR SERVICE TO HIM AND OTHERS?

SOME PEOPLE LIKE TO SET ASIDE A WEEKEND EACH YEAR TO HAVE A PRAYER "RETREAT"—A TIME TO BE ALONE WITH GOD IN PRAYER. MAYBE YOU AREN'T ABLE TO SPEND THAT AMOUNT OF TIME, BUT WHAT ABOUT ONE FULL HOUR AWAY FROM DISTRACTIONS AND CELL PHONES TO JUST PRAY? CALL A BABYSITTER, PACK A SNACK, AND HEAD FOR A PARK OR CHAPEL TODAY.

PRAYER

God of the universe, I'm amazed that You speak to us so quietly and so often. Please soften my heart and give me ears to hear You today.

EXPRESSING LOVE

IT'S NOT ENOUGH TO FEEL LOVE FOR THE SIGNIFICANT OTHERS IN OUR LIVES, WE MUST EXPRESS IT IN OUR WORDS AND ACTIONS.

There is a time for risky love. There is a time for extravagant gestures. There is a time to pour out your affections on one you love. And when the time comes—seize it, don't miss it.

MAX LUCADO

 TO THINK ABOUT

- ⚷ Why does our society struggle so much to express affirmation and affection?
- ⚷ Would your friends and family members describe you as warm and affirming, or cool and aloof?
- ⚷ Are there some ways you can better express love to the important people in your life?

LESSON FOR LIFE

Promises

God will:

Perfect His love in you

1 John 4:12

Use you to

build up others

Ephesians 4:15-16

Love others through you

1 Thessalonians 3:12

Searching for True Love

BIBLE STUDY PASSAGE: 1 JOHN 4

Do all these things; but most important, love each other.
Love is what holds you all together in perfect unity.

COLOSSIANS 3:14

There are a million songs on the airwaves that talk about love. But many of us don't feel very loved. Romance is woven into movies, TV shows, novels—even commercials—and yet there is far too little real affection among couples.

How do you do at expressing love to those significant others in your life? Children? Spouse? Neighbors? Extended family members? Some reminders might be in order—

- True love takes the initiative: "In this is love, not that we loved God, but that He loved us and sent His Son to be the propitiation for our sins" (1 John 4:10 NKJV). God gave us the pattern for loving others: Make the first move.
- True love is active: "My children, we should love people not only with words and talk, but by our actions and true caring" (1 John 3:18). Our culture obsesses over the emotions and

romantic feelings of love. But true love is practical. If your neighbor is hungry, take him or her some food.

- True love is kind: "Love is not rude, is not selfish, and does not get upset with others" (1 Corinthians 13:5). Words may not be enough, but they still matter tremendously. Do your children go to sleep with your final "I love you" of the day echoing in their hearts? Don't make people guess how you feel about them. Tell them!

- True love looks to the needs of others: "Do not be interested only in your own life, but be interested in the lives of others" (Philippians 2:4). All of us need affirmation in our own lives, too. But don't wait around to get what you need before you give others what they need. The good news is that God has a way of blessing you in greater measure than you bless others.

Share with your world the love that God has shared with you. ➤

Don't ever forget kindness and truth. Wear them like a necklace. Write them on your heart as if on a tablet.
Proverbs 3:3

REAL LIFE

Whispers in the Night

JOAN CLAYTON

He first saw me in front of a grocery store—a thirteen-year old fat girl wearing ugly glasses and eating an ice cream cone. That this tall, lanky, handsome kid would even notice me made me believe in miracles. He smiled at me and I smiled back thinking, *Is he really looking at me?*

At fifteen we sat with each other at the Saturday afternoon movies. We saw "Hopalong Cassidy" two or three times.

Our senior year, he asked me to the junior-senior banquet. It took me all day to get ready. My heart thumped when I heard the doorbell. I opened the door to see the most handsome man in the universe with a corsage in his hand.

The day after graduation, Emmitt's letter from Uncle Sam took him off to war. We both cried. His love letters soothed my heart until his tenure finally ended.

After my college graduation, we married, and that's when the whispers in the night began. I can't begin to count how many whispers of "I love you" wafted in my ear. The whispers increased after the births of each of our three sons as Emmitt jumped out of bed when they cried in the night. Many times, I saw him bending down to whisper in little boys' ears as he tucked them back in bed with an "I love you."

Sometimes we woke up with those little boys in bed with us. Imagine my delight when they started whispering in our ears, "I love you" on those sweet mornings.

The boys are grown now with babes of their own. I have the "warm fuzzies" when I see them whispering in their children's ears.

"Daddy, I love you too, but your whiskers tickle!" The giggles and screams of my little granddaughters running down the hall fill our house with joy.

"Gotcha!" Our son swoops up two little girls in his big, strong arms, and the whispering begins again.

I have always whispered to God, but now I'm a "wife whisperer" and a "grandmother whisperer" too. My heart is filled with warm love when I hear my children and grandchildren whisper at the end of their phone call, "I love you, Mawmaw."

Through the many years, my marriage has been sustained by these whispers. Whatever the problem—sick babies, low finances, surgeries, misunderstandings, job stresses, or any other circumstances—they all faded away with arms that held me close and whispers in my ear at night. Whispers of love between Emmitt and me let each other know we would always be here, no matter what.

The journey of life is not always easy, and it requires patience, courage, faith, and most of all, love. ⇒

ACTION STEP

YOUR ASSIGNMENT FOR THIS SOUL MATTER IS SIMPLE. EVERY DAY FOR THE NEXT FIVE DAYS, YOU NEED TO—

- SAY "I LOVE YOU" TO FIVE DIFFERENT PEOPLE.
- HUG FIVE PEOPLE.

PRAYER

Father, thank You for lavishing Your love on us with both words and amazing, incredible actions. Help me express love to the people in my life today.

EVEN MOTHERS NEED A MOTHER

WE ARE BLESSED AS WE MAINTAIN— OR BUILD—OUR RELATIONSHIP WITH OUR MOTHER (OR MOTHER FIGURE).

What do girls do who haven't any mothers
to help them through their troubles?

LOUISA MAY ALCOTT

TO THINK ABOUT

- ✦ What kind of relationship did you and your mother have as you grew up?
- ✦ How has that relationship changed? Is it better? Closer? Has it suffered?
- ✦ Do you know how much your mom loves you? Does she know how much you love her?

LESSON FOR LIFE

Promises

God will:

Always love you

Romans 8:39

Send others to

help you grow

1 Corinthians 4:17

Shield and protect you

Psalm 33:20

Comfort you like

a mother

Isaiah 66:13

A Mother's Love Is Forever

BIBLE STUDY PASSAGE: 1 THESSALONIANS 2

Like babies you will be nursed and held in my arms and bounced on my knees.

ISAIAH 66:12

Most biblical historians—with a few notable exceptions—agree that Paul was a single man. He never makes reference to a wife or children, and his dangerous and adventurous missionary travels would have precluded him from having a significant relationship. Maybe that's why he was such a good "parent" to his "baby" churches, sometimes sounding like a stern father, but often taking the role of a tender mother:

> *We were very gentle with you, like a mother caring for her little children. Because we loved you, we were happy to share not only God's Good News with you, but even our own lives. You had become so dear to us! (1 Thessalonians 2:7-8).*

Paul later wrote to his young protégé, Timothy, and told him to never forget the heritage of faith that was his through his mother and grandmother (2 Timothy 1:5). He counseled him:

> Since you were a child you have known the
> Holy Scriptures which are able to make you wise
> (2 Timothy 3:15).

If you have a loving, intimate, spiritual relationship with your own mom, you are truly a blessed mother. You already know the help and support that can make your days and challenges as a mother easier to manage. If you don't have a close and loving relationship with your mother, however, don't lose heart. Ask God to help you reach out to her with forgiveness, kindness, and grace. And then trust Him to do the rest. If she doesn't respond, or if you have lost your mother to death, also be aware that God can bless you through other women who are older and wiser. Maybe you need to join a weekly Bible study group where you can experience the concern and care of a mother figure.

And never forget, the God whom we refer to as "Father" also comes to us as a "Mother:" "I will comfort you as a mother comforts her child" (Isaiah 66:13). ➡

When Jesus saw his mother and the follower he loved standing nearby, he said to his mother, "Dear woman, here is your son." Then he said to the follower, "Here is your mother." From that time on, the follower took her to live in his home.

John 19:25-27

REAL LIFE

Motherly Love

MICHELE STARKEY

Our mother's love started when we were babies, and carried us into adulthood. But I've found that I've never quite outgrown my need for my mother's nurture and affection.

When I was in my forties, an aneurysm ruptured deep within my brain. As I lay semi-comatose in a hospital some sixty miles from her home, my mother made the trip each morning to sit at my bedside.

Every day, amid the whirl of machines and tubes that connected to every part of my body, she found a spot to place her hands on me. The same loving hands that cradled me as a baby, now frail from the weathering of life, still possessed that unmistakable motherly love.

In my comatose state, I could tell the difference between the gentle nudging of the nurse's hands and the warmth of my mother's hands. My mother's voice would lift the veil that separates the conscious from the unconscious world and I can still hear her prayers encouraging me, "Do not be afraid. God is in control." A mother hopes against all odds and trusts God in all circumstances. She would not give up hope for my recovery.

Many times during her visits, she cradled my face in her hands as if rocking me gently. The nurses in the ICU ward remarked that my blood pressure actually dropped to a more appropriate level when my mother was in the room. Just as a mother seems to be the only one to comfort their child, my adult brain seemed to sense the comfort offered by my mother's heart.

Six weeks passed before I was released from the hospital and sent home to recuperate. Her hands held mine as I took each tender step toward healing. My mother visited me every day after that, and her love reinforced my full recovery. After all, I am her baby, no matter how old I may be.

Through the years, everything that I ever needed to know about love I learned from my mother. Her simple steadfast faith and unwavering love has carried me through the trials in my life—before and since my aneurysm— always caressing me with her mother's touch, that loving warmth that was recognizable even when my eyes were closed.

This kind of motherly love knows no bounds, demands nothing in return, and simply loves for the purpose of loving. It is selfless love. It is the closest comparison to Christ-like love that one can ever imagine. It flows out of a mother's heart. ➤

ACTION STEP

WRITE YOUR MOM A LETTER THANKING HER FOR HER LOVE. BE SPECIFIC ABOUT THE WAYS SHE TOUCHED YOUR LIFE AS YOU WERE GROWING UP AS WELL AS THE WAYS SHE CONTINUES TO BLESS YOU. IF SHE'S STILL ALIVE, SEND IT TO HER. IF NOT, TAKE A MOMENT TO REMEMBER HER AND ALLOW YOURSELF TO GRIEVE AND CELEBRATE THE WAY GOD USED HER TO BLESS YOU.

PRAYER

Lord, I'm always striving to be a great mother. Please make me a great daughter, too! Help me be a blessing to my mom today.

A JOY FOR LIFE

JOY IS BOTH A GIFT
FROM GOD AND A DECISION.

*Slow down and enjoy life. It's not only the scenery
you miss by going too fast—you also miss the
sense of where you are going and why.*

EDDIE CANTOR

TO THINK ABOUT

- How would the people in your life characterize you in terms of joy?
- What are the cares of life that rob you of a sense of joy?
- What can you do to foster a spirit of joy in your life?

LESSON FOR LIFE

Promises

God will:

Produce joy in your life

Galatians 5:22

Renew the joy
of salvation
Psalm 51:12

Deliver you from worry
Philippians 4:6-7

Turn sadness into joy
Psalm 30:11

Abundant Joy

BIBLE STUDY PASSAGE: MATTHEW 6

I pray that the God who gives hope will fill you with much joy and peace while you trust in him.

ROMANS 15:13

The religious leaders of Jesus' day just didn't know what to make of this traveling rabbi who increasingly drew crowds everywhere He visited to teach. One of their main objections was the company He kept—"he is a friend of tax collectors and sinners" (Matthew 11:19). They did not like that He attended feasts and parties (Luke 5:33). He didn't make a show of fasting, praying, and giving—and in fact criticized the Pharisees for their grandiose public displays of piety (Matthew 23:13-33).

The reality is that Jesus did fast (Luke 4:2); He did pray with intensity (Mark 1:35); He did caution His disciples about their activities and priorities (Matthew 5:29, 6:1); but Jesus adamantly taught that life is wonderful and to be enjoyed: "The friends of the bridegroom do not give up eating while the bridegroom is still with them" (Mark 2:19).

In fact, in contrast to the doom and gloom teaching of His

day, He says: "I have come that they may have life, and that they may have it more abundantly" (John 10:10).

All throughout Scripture, we are reminded—actually, we are commanded—to be joyful:

- "Be joyful in the Lord your God" (Joel 2:23).
- "Serve the Lord with joy; come before him with singing" (Psalm 100:2).
- "In the world you will have tribulation; but be of good cheer, I have overcome the world" (John 16:33 NKJV).
- "Be full of joy in the Lord always" (Philippians 4:4).

It doesn't seem like we should need to be told to be joyful. And yet the human condition makes it very tempting for us to sink into anger, resentment, self-pity, and complaining. Think of the people in your own life. How many are truly joyful?

One of the great gifts you can give to yourself—and your children—is the gift of joy. Ask God to plant the seeds of joy in your heart. And then determine to enjoy life to the fullest. ➡

You give us wine that makes happy hearts and olive oil that makes our faces shine. You give us bread that gives us strength.
Psalm 104:15

REAL LIFE

NASCAR Mama

DIANE H. PITTS

"Mom, is this the week we race at Mr. Haynes's house?" Tyler, our eleven-year-old, popped his head around the door with an expectant grin on his face. With an impatient roar I fired back, "I hope not. Nothing ever gets done around here, and now this NASCAR fixation wrecks our Saturdays." Immediately Tyler's excitement fizzled. He walked away dejectedly.

My conscience nudged me, but I mentally defended my attitude. After all, I had returned to work to help resolve our family's debts, making time a precious commodity in our house. Besides, it was my husband who had encouraged me to rejoin the workforce, and my earnings had partly bankrolled their NASCAR endeavors. The crush of work, school, home, and carpool was wearing me out, and they didn't seem to care.

Still stewing, I worked through mounds of laundry, put together a Sunday school lesson, and cooked all at the same time. Grumbling, I watched as my husband and three boys loaded the go-cart onto his truck, laughing and talking.

"They have all the fun," I muttered. Why did they have it so easy? Didn't they understand how stressed I was trying to keep things together?

As the day wore on, all I could think about was how much I had to do—and how my husband and kids were off having a good time. Resentment began to bubble in my heart until finally, in exasperation, I drove down to the local dirt track to give them some racing cues they would never forget.

My Explorer bumped along our friend's driveway until the track came into view. What I saw made me pull over immediately. There on the track were the men in our neighborhood, having the time of their lives. These guys drove with abandon, their children cheering every lap.

My hardworking husband, who never asked for anything, was connecting with his sons and the other men. Wives and moms were present, enjoying conversation, sights, and sounds. Taking in the scene, I slowly drove away.

I had neglected to report my need for maintenance to the crew. Instead of enjoying life with my boys, I'd gotten bogged down with tasks. I needed a break. I still had some things to do that afternoon, but decided I could probably wrap those up quickly and be ready to spend time with my guys when they returned home. We would all be winners today, and especially the next time around.

The day I resolved to take a much needed pit stop from the cares of life to enjoy the exhilarating race of life with my husband and kids was the day my burdens were lightened. And this mom who didn't know a spark plug from an exhaust pipe allowed racing to become a high octane fuel for joy in my family. ➤

ACTION STEP

DISCIPLINE AND DUTY ARE WONDERFUL TRAITS. BECAUSE OF THIS, ONE COMMON SUGGESTION AMONG EFFICIENCY EXPERTS IS THAT WE SHOULD TACKLE OUR LEAST PLEASANT TASKS OF THE DAY FIRST, THEN MOVE TO EASIER, MORE PLEASANT CHORES. WHY NOT TURN THAT UPSIDE DOWN FOR A WEEK?

WRITE AN AGENDA FOR EACH DAY—ALWAYS PUTTING FUN ACTIVITIES FIRST. FOR FAMILY MEALS, BEGIN WITH DESSERT, THEN MOVE TO THE MAIN COURSE. THIS MAY NOT BE A REALISTIC PLAN OVER TIME, BUT HAVE FUN WITH IT TODAY!

PRAYER

Father God, I know You want me to be joyful. Help me cast my cares on You and enjoy the family You've given me.

SAVORING THE MOMENT

CHILDREN GROW UP MORE QUICKLY THAN WE CAN IMAGINE— ENJOY EACH DAY AS A GIFT.

At the end of your life, you will never regret not having passed one more test, not winning one more verdict, or not closing one more deal. You will regret time not spent with a husband, a friend, a child or a parent.

BARBARA BUSH

TO THINK ABOUT

- Are you ever tempted to spend more time in the future or past than you do in the now?
- Do you savor the life you have right now or wish for something different?
- Why is patience so tough in today's world?

LESSON FOR LIFE

This Is the Day

BIBLE STUDY PASSAGE: PSALM 103

Go and enjoy good food and sweet drinks. Send some to people who have none, because today is a holy day to the Lord. Don't be sad, because the joy of the Lord will make you strong.

NEHEMIAH 8:10

Some of us dwell too much on the past. *Things were so much better then*, or *If only this had worked out differently.*

Some of us dwell too much on the future. *Things will be different then*, or *Oh no, I don't know what's going to happen.*

The psalmist declares: "This is the day that the Lord has made. Let us rejoice and be glad today!" (Psalm 118:24).

So whether your temptation is impatience for or worry about tomorrow, or regrets about or longing for yesterday, one secret of living a blessed life is enjoying and savoring today.

But I have two kids in diapers. We're having a tough time financially. My teen is driving me crazy. I hate that we moved and wish we could be back with our old friends.

To savor today does not mean that everything is perfect. It

doesn't mean you shouldn't have aspirations and dreams for you and your family. It does mean you will never have today again. From a prison cell, Paul wrote: "I have learned the secret of being happy at any time in everything that happens, when I have enough to eat and when I go hungry, when I have more than I need and when I do not have enough. I can do all things through Christ, because he gives me strength" (Philippians 4:12-13).

In fact, Paul relates how we spend our time today with salvation when he writes: "See then that you walk circum-spectly, not as fools but as wise, redeeming the time, because the days are evil" (Ephesians 5:15-16 NKJV).

Each day is a gift from God to be lived fully and savored. Nothing will bless you and your children more than to love where you are in life. So carpe diem—"seize the day"—and thank God for who you are in Him. ➤

A happy heart is like a continual feast.
Proverbs 15:15

REAL LIFE

An Important Message

TEENA STEWART

I pulled up into my usual spot along the curb where I would wait for the final school bell. Soon my lanky son, my youngest child, would be belched forth from the bowels of the school along with hundreds of other children.

After our move to California, we learned that our small town did not provide school bus service. So every afternoon I had to stop what I was doing and sit by the curb for fifteen to twenty minutes and wait.

Waiting is not something I do well.

Still, I had become accustomed to the waiting. In just a few months my son would be in college, and I'd recently come to see the daily trip as something more than an inconvenience—it was an opportunity to connect with my teen for a few precious minutes and to take a badly needed break from the grind.

As the sun beat through the dusty windshield, I noticed a hand-written label in the corner of the back window of the minivan in front of me. The note read simply, PATIENT.

"PATIENT," I mouthed softly, wondering. Was it a warning? Had the person in the van escaped from a mental institution? I grinned at the mental image of me hurriedly locking my car doors.

As I studied the writing, another possibility clambered to the front of my foggy brain. Maybe it was a subtle reminder from God that I should be patient.

It certainly seemed like the most feasible meaning considering my life's current state of affairs.

I didn't particularly like the way my life had been unfolding recently. First, there were the muddled family finances and the error my husband had discovered after having someone new fill out our income taxes. Then, in an attempt to help out, I had been scurrying to land some higher-paying writing jobs. But my efforts weren't panning out—I had spent money I didn't have on advertising with minimal results.

Then came my son's upcoming college expenses. The cost of living in our area was already bleeding us dry. How were we going to come up with tuition? Were we supposed to open a vein? The thought had occurred to me that I would have been better off if I had simply done nothing and—waited.

I'd grown increasingly angry with God, and my cynical attitude was beginning to show. I guess He knew I needed the sign. It was as plain as day, like someone leaving a casual message on the dry erase board by the phone.

As my son slid into the passenger seat, I put the car in gear, anxious to get back to work.

PATIENT, the sign reminded.

I eased off the accelerator and took my time going home. There would be so few trips like this left. If it was important enough for Him to send such a visible reminder, maybe I'd better listen. "Take things at a slower pace," He seemed to be saying. "Learn to trust Me and rest in today." ➤

ACTION STEP

TAKE TIME TODAY TO STOP AND SMELL THE ROSES. ON A SMALL PIECE OF PAPER OR NOTECARD, DO A LITTLE ARTWORK WITH CRAYON OR MARKER OR EVEN PAINT—MAYBE SOME SMALL RED ROSES OR A CARTOON PORTRAIT OF YOUR FAMILY OR AN ARTFUL RENDERING OF A FAVORITE BIBLE VERSE—AND POST IT SOMEWHERE AS A REMINDER TO SAVOR YOUR LIFE TODAY.

PRAYER

Lord God, You've given me a great life. Give me a fresh delight in Your gifts and creation, and teach my kids through me that Your plan and timing are wonderful.

EMPTY NEST SYNDROME

IT IS HEALTHY TO MOURN—AND CELEBRATE— WHEN CHILDREN LEAVE THE HOME.

*When mothers talk about the depression of the empty nest,
they're not mourning the passing of all those wet towels on the
floor, or the music that numbs your teeth, or even the bottle
of capless shampoo dribbling down the shower drain. They're
upset because they've gone from supervisor of a child's life to a
spectator. It's like being the vice president of the United States.*

ERMA BOMBECK

 ## TO THINK ABOUT

- What do you most dread about having no more children in the home?
- What do you most look forward to about the last child leaving home?
- What are you doing now to build an adult relationship with your children?

LESSON FOR LIFE

Promises

God will:

Never leave you alone

Hebrews 13:5

Be close to you

Isaiah 41:10

Psalm 27:10

Give you a sense

of purpose

Acts 20:24

Give you new tasks

Ephesians 2:10

A New Thing

BIBLE STUDY PASSAGE: ISAIAH 40

Look at the new thing I am going to do. It is already
happening. Don't you see it? I will make a road in the
desert and rivers in the dry land.

ISAIAH 43:19

Life is filled with changes, including the blessed—and
sometimes painful—reality that our children are growing up
and will someday leave the house. (There are a few of us
counting the days to that event with anticipation!)

The teen years and your child's natural transition toward
greater levels of independence, hopefully done in a healthy and
positive manner, will help your own transition of saying
goodbye. It is not uncommon, however, to cling and hold on
tight when the end is in sight.

Some scriptures that will help you face the challenges of
change—and change can be painful—include:
- "There is a time for everything, and everything on earth
  has its special season" (Ecclesiastes 3:1). God created
  the seasons of life, including the moment when a child

138

flies from the protective nest called home.

- Not only is God preparing new tasks and planting new dreams for your kids, but He is doing something new in your life. Simply breathe the prayer, "What's next for me, God?" Now look forward to hearing the answer.

- "For God is my witness, how greatly I long for you all with the affection of Jesus Christ" (Romans 1:11 NKJV). Whether your child is off to a nearby dorm room, getting married and moving across town, or leaving for a country halfway around the globe, you will always need and love each other. Find new ways to communicate and stay close.

- "Then you will be perfect and complete and will have everything you need" (James 1:4). Just as James desired maturity and independence for his "baby Christians," so you too, if you look deep in your heart, desire your children to have the ability to be independent from you.

An empty nest might be looming right around the corner for you—or years away. Today, simply celebrate that your children are growing! ➤

Even when you are old, I will be the same. Even when your hair has turned gray, I will take care of you. I made you and will take care of you. I will carry you and save you.

Isaiah 46:4

REAL LIFE

Does the Nest Really Empty?

LINDA GILDEN

I stood in the doorway of Kristi's room. Her teddy bear rested his head on the pillow of her unmade bed. On the floor under my feet was a yellow card. "Request for Name Change," it read, "Social Security Office."

Kristi had been married less than twenty-four hours. With a few brief words, she had gone from sleeping with her teddy bear to sleeping with her husband. With a stamped postcard, she would leave maidenhood behind—name and all—and henceforth be known as Mrs.

It seemed like just moments ago that she had called and said, "Get everybody on the phone. I have something to tell you! I'm getting married!"

Over twenty years ago, when I first looked at my precious daughter, I not only thanked God for her, but also began to pray for the man she would marry. I had a wonderful husband, and I knew that he was part of God's plan for my life. I wanted the same for my daughter when the time came for a young man to ask for her hand in marriage. Now that time had come.

As she crossed this threshold into married life, I too was crossing a new threshold. How would I ever fill this empty spot in my nest?

The writer of Ecclesiastes notes that, "There is a time for everything, and everything on earth has its special season." In the same moment my daughter had gone from maiden to matron, I had gone from mother to mother-in-law and friend. I wasn't sure what this season was going to bring. I wasn't even sure I was prepared for this season.

However, it didn't take me long to realize the scripture was right. This season wasn't so bad. The role of mother-in-law and friend had a lot of potential for fun. I loved sharing recipes and offering words of encouragement and going on impromptu shopping trips. It was especially fun to double date!

I'm finding that the empty nest syndrome is like some other things in life— a bit over dramatized! Every milestone creates a change, and sometimes we cling to things we think are the best they could possibly be. But God wouldn't take something good away from us unless He had something equally good or better in mind.

As I look back to that post-wedding morning, I remember despairing that my "nest" would never be the same. But I really am enjoying my new role as the mother bird in the empty nest. My husband and I have begun to date again. I can sleep a little later if I want to. And even though the baby birds are flying, they often revisit the nest.

Yes, the empty nest is not so bad, and it doesn't stay empty long. It seems ours might be in for a refill—this morning, as I walked across the family room, I tripped over the leg of the new baby swing my husband set up for our first granddaughter's visit. ➢

ACTION STEP

ONE OF THE LOST PARENTING TRADITIONS IS FILLING A "HOPE CHEST." THE IDEA IS SIMPLE: BUY A LARGE WOODEN CHEST, AND EACH YEAR BUY ONE PRACTICAL ITEM FOR YOUR CHILD TO SET UP THEIR OWN HOME—DISHES, FLATWARE, TOWELS, AND OTHER MUCH-NEEDED ITEMS.

MAYBE THIS ACTIVITY FEELS TOO INVOLVED, BUT THERE ARE OTHER WAYS TO CREATE A "SEND-OFF" PRESENT, LIKE AN EACH-YEAR PHOTO ALBUM. GET CREATIVE AND COME UP WITH YOUR OWN PLAN FOR SENDING YOUR CHILDREN INTO THE WORLD WITH PRACTICAL TOOLS, FAITH, AND MEMORIES.

PRAYER

Lord, I know that You will never leave me, and that Your plans for me are good. Help me see You in the season of life I'm in right now.

BUILDING GOOD MEMORIES

ONE OF THE GREATEST GIFTS YOU CAN GIVE TO YOUR CHILDREN IS WONDERFUL MEMORIES OF FUN TIMES SPENT TOGETHER.

God gave us memories that we might have roses in December.

J.M. BARRIE

 TO THINK ABOUT

- Why are sweet memories so important in the big picture of life?
- What are some of your special memories from your own childhood?
- What memories are you planting in your children's heart?

LESSON FOR LIFE

Promises

God will:

Give you good things

Psalm 84:11

Be with you as you get
together with others

Matthew 18:20

Give you good times
with friends and family

Psalm 55:14

Green Pastures

BIBLE STUDY PASSAGE: PSALM 23

*I remember what happened long ago; I consider every-
thing you have done. I think about all you have made.*

PSALM 143:5

There are three steps to building memories with your children—

- You have to do something fun and significant with them—
  which means spending time with them. No wonder kids
  spell love, T-I-M-E. Whether planned or spontaneous, a
  passive approach to life will not build great memories. If
  you're stuck in a state of personal inertia, it's time to get
  up and start moving. "But be doers of the word, and not
  hearers only, deceiving yourselves" (James 1:22 NKJV).
- You have to interpret and take note of what just happened.
  Two families driving along the same highway can have
  totally different experiences. One family frowns in stony
  silence, bored, preoccupied, and oblivious to the world
  around them. The second family, on the other hand,
  plays games, notices baby sheep next to mommies, and

talks to each other. You have to explain to your children that something significant is going on— even when it's only a family dinner on a Sunday afternoon or going to the park on a Tuesday evening. Just before the Israelites celebrated Passover before entering the Promised Land, the Lord explained to Joshua and the people: "As slaves in Egypt you were ashamed, but today I have removed that shame." (Joshua 5:9). He wanted them to understand something amazing was going on.

- You need to create mementos and markers. Memories fade. That's why photo albums, scrapbooks, and creative memory notebooks are so important. Handprints in concrete, purity rings, marks inside closet doors with heights and dates, junk boxes with old trophies, patches, and certificates all create clutter, but provide memories. One Old Testament tradition was leaving stones at important places when God had delivered: "See this stone! It will remind you of what we did today. It was here the Lord spoke to us today" (Joshua 24:27).

Just as the Gentle Shepherd leads you into "green pastures" of good memories (Psalm 23:2), so you too can lead your children to experience joy and wonder to last a lifetime. ➤

He has made everything beautiful in its time.

Ecclesiastes 3:11 NKJV

REAL LIFE

Half the Fun Is Getting There

JANET LYNN MITCHELL

It never crossed our minds that we were doing something outrageous. Although it was summer vacation, both of our husbands had to work. Yet Annette, pregnant and showing, and I, with an injured knee, decided to take our kids and get away. With five children under the age of seven, we knew our trip would not be lacking adventure.

We packed the van carefully. With sleeping bags, five squirt guns, junk food, and the latest chick flick that had hit the market, we headed towards the mountains. Even with "Veggie Tales" playing in the background, it wasn't long until our crew became restless.

"He's touching me!"

"He has to touch you—we're packed in here like sardines."

"How long until we get there?"

"Hey," Annette said in her teacher voice. "Half the fun is getting there!"

A couple of hours later, we rounded the mountain and soon stood on the doorsteps of Oakhaven, my parents' mountain home.

"Who's got the key?" one of the kids hollered.

The key! Oh no! In the midst of packing the van, I had set the key down on my kitchen counter. I had forgotten the key. Immediately I said a quick prayer. Then grabbing Annette's arm, I whispered in her ear, "Remember you said half the fun is getting there? Well, we're not inside yet, and the key is at home on my kitchen counter!"

Quickly turning our situation into a game, Annette, the kids, and I began rattling all doors and checking all windows for a way inside.

"Look here!" Annette shouted. "The kitchen window above the sink doesn't have a safety lock. Janet, if you hoist me up, I can open the window and crawl through."

"You can what? You're pregnant!"

"Well, you can't do it. You've got a bad knee."

Before I knew it, all five kids stood cheering, watching Annette crawling though the window while I braced her. As Annette's feet disappeared from sight, one of her kids shouted, "Mom, remember: Half the fun is getting there!"

We had a great time during our vacation at Oakhaven. The kids laughed, played, hiked, and even learned to whistle through an acorn. Annette and I found the time to talk like schoolgirls, and late one night when the kids were tucked in bed, we curled up and watched our chick flick.

Looking back to the days when Annette and I so daringly headed for the mountains with our little brood, we both smile. For now we know for certain that half the fun of motherhood is sharing it with a friend. →

ACTION STEP

TO MAKE TODAY A SPECIAL DAY IN YOUR CHILDREN'S MEMORIES AND CULTIVATE A SENSE OF WONDER AND JOY, PLAN A WALK IN THE WOODS. YOU OBVIOUSLY NEED TO CONSIDER THE AGES OF YOUR CHILDREN WHEN DETERMINING THE KIND OF TERRAIN YOU WILL EXPLORE AND THE DISTANCE OF YOUR WALK. BUT GET AS FAR AWAY FROM THE ORDINARY AS YOU CAN ON A DAY TRIP.

IF YOUR CHILDREN ARE YOUNGER, PROVIDE THEM WITH A BAG TO "COLLECT" THINGS THAT INTEREST THEM. THEY WILL LOVE THIS PART OF YOUR ACTIVITY EVEN IF ALL THEY PICK UP ARE TWIGS AND ROCKS. FOR OLDER CHILDREN AND TEENS (AND YOURSELF) SUPPLY A JOURNAL. TOWARD THE END OF THE DAY, SET ASIDE TIME TO WRITE DOWN IMPRESSIONS OF GOD'S CREATION—AND A PRAYER OF THANKSGIVING FOR THE WONDERFUL WORLD AND BEAUTIFUL TODAY HE HAS MADE.

PRAYER

Heavenly Father, You have given me so many good gifts. Help me to always remember Your goodness.

TIME WITH GOD

IN THE HUSTLE AND BUSTLE OF LIFE, WE NEED STILL, QUIET MOMENTS TO BE ALONE WITH GOD.

Every morning I spend fifteen minutes filling my mind full of God; and so there's no room left for worry thoughts.

HOWARD CHANDLER CHRISTY

TO THINK ABOUT

- ☞ How often do you experience "quietness" in your life? How much is on purpose?
- ☞ What are the biggest distractions in your life?
- ☞ How would your life change if you spent even a little time each day in silent reflection?

LESSON FOR LIFE

Promises

God will:

Be near you
Psalm 145:18

Give you unlimited
access to Him
Ephesians 3:12

Bear your burdens
Matthew 11:28-29

Give you rest
Psalm 23:2

Away from the Crowds

BIBLE STUDY PASSAGE: JOHN 4:1-11

Pray in the Spirit at all times with all kinds of prayers, asking for everything you need. To do this you must always be ready and never give up. Always pray for all God's people.

EPHESIANS 6:18

If you read through the four Gospels you can't help but notice how people—and crowds—were drawn to Jesus. If He went up a hill to pray alone, the crowds would be gathered below awaiting His return (Luke 4:42). If He jumped into a boat to slip off to the other side of a lake, word of His movements would race Him to the other side (Matthew 14:13). He interacted non-stop with military officers, widows, children, the seriously ill, the demon-possessed, religious leaders, close friends, prophets, and sinners.

At the beginning of His ministry at age thirty, despite having so much to do in such a short amount of time for His Father in heaven, Jesus pulled away from everyone to spend forty days in the wilderness to pray and fast. While alone, Jesus was tested three times by Satan, but each time answered the challenge with scripture and a profound sense of His purpose in life (Matthew 4:1-11).

Again, at the end of His earthly life, Jesus pulled away from the crowds to pray alone in the Garden of Gethsemane (Mark 14:35-36). It was there, with the agony of the cross just before Him, that He reaffirmed His most earnest desire: "Not My will, but Yours, be done" (Luke 22:42 NKJV).

If Jesus Christ sought solitude and quiet, how much more important is it for us? We can come to the end of the day—or week or even month—and discover that we made no time at all to be alone with God. Television, ball practice, chores, children's arguments, and a cacophony of other "noises" crowd out prayer and silent reflection.

You don't have to take a forty-day trip to the desert to create ways to spend quiet time alone with God. You might have to enlist some support in taking care of the kids for a while, but your soul will thrive as you pull away from the noise to hear the voice of your Father. ➡

The Lord is close to everyone who prays to him, to all who truly pray to him.

Psalm 145:18

 **REAL LIFE**

A Sunshine Day

GLENDA PALMER

I glanced at the paper magnetized to the refrigerator: "High School Beach Party Saturday 10-3."

I'd better run—it's almost three now, I thought.

As I drove to the church, random thoughts about the rest of the day filled my mind: *I've got to go to the grocery store before dinner. I wonder if Jeannie remembered her flute lesson...*

I pulled in a parking space in front of the church. Just as I'd suspected: They weren't back yet, and I didn't even bring anything to read.

Ten minutes later, I was becoming more uncomfortable in the hot car. If the church auditorium was open, I could get a drink of cold water, I mused.

I looked down at my old denim shorts and faded top and hoped no one saw me.

I got out, walked up the cement stairs, and tried the huge front door. *That's lucky,* I thought as the door opened easily. Strolling across the foyer to the drinking fountain, I glanced briefly into the dark auditorium.

The icy water tasted good, and the air in the building sure was cooler than in my stifling car. I wondered if anyone else was around.

"Hello?" No one answered, so I walked into the auditorium. I had never been in the church when it was dark and empty. It had always been filled with nicely-dressed worshipers, angelic choir members, and kind ushers. It was so silent and dim now—except for a bright spot of light shining right on the center pews.

I wondered where the light was coming from—it looked like it was coming from the balcony. I walked slowly down the aisle looking back to see if I could find the source.

"Wow, look at that! Oh, how beautiful—how beautiful," I breathed.

The small balcony was aglow with a rainbow of colors. The ceiling, floor, pews, songbooks, and even my faded white shirt were covered with bright reds, blues, yellows, and greens as the sunlight shone through each piece of leaded glass. As I tiptoed over to the window and touched its warmth, I gazed at the blood-red reflection on my hand. Swallowing, I looked at the simple cross in the center with rows of varied-colored glass jewels framing it. Each tiny piece of hand-blown glass had been carefully cut and set in its own place to make a glorious, complete picture.

Alone in the silence, I knelt and whispered, "Oh, Lord, thank You for meeting with me here today. Forgive me for being too busy with worldly things to see Your sacrifice and majesty every day. Remind me so I never forget. Amen."

Outside I could hear the squeaking brakes and loud, laughing teenagers. I took a deep breath and a last look at my stained glass window. Reluctantly I walked down the stairs.

A sandy, smiling boy was standing by the car with his surfboard and towel.

"It was great, Mom, and the waves were awesome!"

"I had an awesome day, too." ➤

ACTION STEP

FASTING IS THE SPIRITUAL DISCIPLINE OF NOT PARTAKING OF FOOD FOR A SET PERIOD OF TIME IN ORDER TO DEVOTE OUR HEARTS AND MINDS TO SPIRITUAL MATTERS. BUT ABSTAINING FROM FOOD IS NOT THE ONLY PHYSICAL EXPRESSION OF FASTING. CONSIDER A ONE-, TWO-, OR THREE-DAY PERIOD OF NO RADIO, TV, OR OTHER "NOISE" IN YOUR HOME. (DISCUSS THIS WITH YOUR FAMILY FIRST!) REMEMBER, THE PURPOSE IS TO FOCUS OUR WHOLE HEART, SOUL, AND MIND ON GOD!

PRAYER

You speak to me through Your Word, and through pastors, and through books, but thank You, God, that You also speak to me in a quiet voice when I am silent before You.

PRAYER

THROUGH PRAYER, GOD HAS PROVIDED A VERY SPECIAL WAY TO RELATE TO HIM AND SHARE OUR LIVES WITH HIM.

*God does not stand afar off as I struggle to speak. He cares
enough to listen with more than casual attention. He translates
my scrubby words and hears what is truly inside. He hears
my sighs and uncertain gropings as fine prose.*

TIMOTHY JONES

TO THINK ABOUT

- Is prayer easy for you or difficult? Do you feel like you're really talking to God?
- What gets in the way of you spending time in prayer? How do you combat distractions?
- How does prayer impact your day-to-day life?

LESSON FOR LIFE

Promises

God will:

Hear your heartfelt
prayers
John 14:14

Know and meet
your needs
Matthew 6:32-33

Reward your persistence
Luke 18:1, 7

Mastering the Basics

BIBLE STUDY PASSAGE: LUKE 11:1-13

When a believing person prays, great things happen.

JAMES 5:16

Prayer is one of the fundamentals of your spiritual life. It can also be one of the most complex and challenging elements in your relationship with God.

The very simplest way to understand prayer is to realize that it is conversation with God. At the heart of prayer is a dialogue with the Creator of the universe. Here are some reminders to take to heart—

- Prayer is God's gracious invitation to you: "So, brothers and sisters, we are completely free to enter the Most Holy Place without fear because of the blood of Jesus' death" (Hebrews 10:19). Mark it on your calendar. You have been invited into the presence of God Almighty. Through Jesus Christ, our great High Priest, you can confidently draw near to God.
- Prayer begins with listening: "Lord, every morning you

hear my voice. Every morning, I tell you what I need, and I wait for your answer" (Psalm 5:3). There is nothing wrong with bringing petitions to God. We are encouraged to do so. However, do you take the time to quiet your heart and listen for God's voice?

- Prayer is empowered through faith: "Anyone who comes to God must believe that he is real and that he rewards those who truly want to find him" (Hebrews 11:6). For prayer to be effective, it must come from a trust and strong belief in God's love for you and His willingness to act in your life.

- Prayer is learned: "One time Jesus was praying in a certain place. When he finished, one of his followers said to him, 'Lord, teach us to pray as John taught his followers'" (Luke 11:1). Prayer may not always come naturally for you. Just like any other discipline in life, it takes practice and patience to develop your praying muscles.

If you find yourself getting discouraged with life and prayer, know that your prayers will be heard and your attempts to strengthen your prayer life will be rewarded. ➔

> For the eyes of the Lord
> are on the righteous,
> And His ears are open
> to their prayers.
>
> 1 Peter 3:12 NKJV

REAL LIFE

God Knows Our Favorite Colors

AUTUMN J. CONLEY

The apartment really wasn't so bad at first. It was an old brick building the locals referred to as "the cow barns"—a reference to its historical use. But the rent was low, it had two bedrooms, and it had a small back yard of sorts.

It had been hard living with my parents in my little brother's old bedroom with my new daughter's baby crib, changing table, and diapers crammed in the corner.

So, the apartment had been an answer to the desperate prayers of a single mom. A place of our own, where we lived for several years, making memories of potty training, first snowmen, and toddler Christmases.

But by the time my daughter was in preschool, the two of us began to realize that it was time to pray for bigger and better things. The Ohio summer days were proving increasingly intolerable (as they don't exactly make air conditioners to fit old cow barn-sized windows), the roof was in such disrepair that we had to put her old baby bathtub in the top of her closet to keep her clothes from getting drenched when it rained, and the back yard, full of broken concrete slabs and shards of glass, was not really a safe play area. What was a perfect answer to my desperate prayers three years earlier was a cause for more desperate prayers now.

My daughter, as young as she was, knew about prayer. She knew that our little two-person family was never really alone. She knew God would take care of us. So I asked Cissy to pray, too, for a new place to live. And she did.

Of course, her prayers were different than mine. She gave God real instructions—a pink room for her, a blue room for Mommy, a bathtub (since she was terrified of our *Psycho*-like shower), and a place where she could learn to ride a bike without getting glass in the tires.

As much as those prayers made me giggle, God took them very seriously. Through a series of life-bettering events, He opened doors for us—front and back doors, garage doors, and closet doors—to a beautiful little storybook house. He used a new job to boost my income and my kind-hearted grandparents as landlords looking for a new tenant. It didn't happen overnight, but it did happen.

On the December day we moved in, the first thing Cissy did was run to the bathroom. "Mommy, there's a real bathtub that doesn't drip!" she exclaimed. She bolted upstairs and excitedly announced, "Mommy, God knows our favorite colors," admiring her room that just so happened to be pink and mine in every shade of blue.

While I know from experience that God answers the desperate prayers of mothers in need, I also know He hears and answers the prayers of our children, giving them their heart's desires. And that is, perhaps, a mother's most heartfelt prayer of all. ➔

ACTION STEP

THIS WEEK, KEEP A LOG OF YOUR PRAYERS. MAKE COLUMNS OR START A NEW PAGE FOR EACH OF THE FOLLOWING PRAYER ELEMENTS:

- PRAISE—SPEAKING WELL OF GOD, REMEMBERING HIS ACTS OF CREATION AND REDEMPTION
- THANKSGIVING—RECOGNIZING AND APPRECIATING WHAT GOD HAS DONE FOR YOU
- CONFESSION—ADMITTING TO GOD AREAS OF SIN IN YOUR LIFE
- PETITION—BRINGING YOUR NEEDS AND CONCERNS TO YOUR LOVING HEAVENLY FATHER
- INTERCESSION—GOING BEFORE GOD ON BEHALF OF SOMEONE ELSE

TRY TO PRAY IN EACH CATEGORY DAILY THIS WEEK.
WARNING: JOURNALING YOUR PRAYERS MAY BECOME ADDICTIVE!

PRAYER

Lord God, I'm in awe that You continually invite me into Your presence in prayer. Help me pray faithfully today.

ANOTHER CHILD?

GOD WILL PROVIDE GUIDANCE
FOR ALL YOUR LIFE DECISIONS
IF YOU ASK WITH FAITH.

Making the decision to have a child is momentous.
It is to decide forever to have your heart
go walking around outside your body.

ELIZABETH STONE

TO THINK ABOUT

- Have you discussed and considered the "ideal" number of kids for your family?
- Are there special blessings to having a larger family? A smaller family?
- Have you prayed about how many kids you should have?

LESSON FOR LIFE

Promises

God will:

Give you wisdom

James 1:5

Bless your family

Deuteronomy 28:4

Help you know
what to do

Psalm 32:8

Give you joy in your
circumstances

James 1:2

Gifts from God

BIBLE STUDY PASSAGE: 1 SAMUEL 1

I prayed for this child, and the Lord answered my prayer and gave him to me. Now I give him back to the Lord. He will belong to the Lord all his life.

1 SAMUEL 1:27-28

The world is so bad today, I don't want to bring another child into it.

Families with strong faith in God need to have large families in order to evangelize the world.

I can't afford the baby I've got, so no way could I handle another.

I think I need to call my husband—we have a surprise on the way.

There are a myriad of views on family size, ranging everywhere from "The world can't sustain any more people, so I'm not having one," to "The more, the merrier."

We need not feel guilt or obligation about "increasing our tribe" on the one hand, but neither should we make this decision only on the basis of practicality.

Consider Hannah. Her heart's desire was to have a child, but after years of marriage, it did not appear that she was physically able to get pregnant. The grief she felt was deep, but was made even worse by the way she was treated by her husband's other wife. In this age when polygamy was still the norm, it was the wife who bore the most children who was often most revered.

In abject grief, Hannah visited the temple and poured out her heart to God. Her crying was so intense that the priest on duty scolded her for being drunk. When she told him the burden of her heart, he prophetically replied back to her, "May the God of Israel give you what you asked of him" (1 Samuel 1:17).

Hannah did have a son. She named him Samuel, which means "asked of God." And true to her word, she offered Samuel back to God with a profound sense of gratitude and an absolute confidence that he was a gift from God. She brought him to the temple where he served God and later became the chief priest of his nation.

You may not pray for and receive a miracle baby like Hannah, but all of us are asked to trust God with every decision in our lives and with our most precious gifts, including our children. ➤

Children are a gift from the Lord; babies are a reward.
Psalm 127:3

REAL LIFE

Wonder-Full

LYNDA BLAIR VERNALIA

My husband and I recently started discussing having a second child. The first time we had this discussion, I ended up spending nine months high on anticipation and exhaustion, and could not sit through Disney's *Tarzan* without wailing like Medea. The last three weeks of my pregnancy, I drove fifty miles an hour over every speed bump available trying to induce labor. (Not to mention that I stood for eight of the thirteen drug-free hours I labored through.)

So what person in her right mind chooses months of nausea followed by months of bingeing? Elects for stomach expansion beyond anything rational? Signs up for classes on how to kiss the body she had in college goodbye? Endures incessant questions: "Do you know the sex? Why not?" Embraces the prospect of swollen feet, fallen arches, and sciatica? Shuns the cat that will no longer be able to lie on top of her belly due to the beach ball expanding therein?

The answer is: no one. Women with biological clock hormones screaming in our ears are not in any sense of "right" mind.

Then why another baby? Could pregnancy have advantages? Some of my friends had several children in rapid succession, wanting to "get it all out of the way" as if they were Christmas shopping in August. Having babies all at once does not get them "out of the way"; that puts multiple inarticulate helpless beings screaming, sneezing, puking, and pushing underfoot.

Of course, pregnancy has its advantages, like a nine-month carte blanche to be demanding, for example. One workday during pregnancy uno, I craved quesadillas, ordering local delivery. The delivery guy decided to take my lunch on tour. I phoned the restaurant an hour later to inform them, "I am pregnant and STARVING!" I then proceeded to call every fifteen minutes regarding my lunch's continued absence until the driver and manager arrived simultaneously. The male driver, unattached, brought me nothing but rubbery cheese between soggy tortillas. The manager, married with children, had a hot, fresh meal in hand, "on the house." Sweet victory!

Also, the option to inflict guilt upon my older child about the sacrifices I made has its merits.

"My feet used to be a size eight!"

"If I spent eight hours standing in labor, you can wait in line fifteen minutes!"

"Enjoy that bikini—while you can."

In all seriousness, I have already decided to have another baby because of one thing: wonder.

There is wonder in a pregnant woman. Inside, kicks and all, that baby is divine. Everyone watches the pregnant woman shifting in line with her golden aura and potential growing inside.

Having four siblings, I know my child should have at least one. She should witness the wonder of a miracle only God can give, and should have the chance to understand that there will be enough window seats in the car, enough turns to go first, even more than enough laughter and love to go around. ⇥

There will be anticipation, exhaustion, crying, guilt, demands—and possibly a cat who will shun me in turn—but a miracle from God can still, in the end, only be wonder-full.

ACTION STEP

IF YOU HAVE ANOTHER BABY ON THE WAY OR PLAN TO SOON, THANK GOD! AND BEGIN NOW TO LET THAT GIFT OF GOD KNOW HOW MUCH YOU LOOK FORWARD TO HIM OR HER. WRITE A "RUNNING" LETTER TO YOUR BABY, DESCRIBING YOUR PREGNANCY, BUT MOST OF ALL YOUR ANTICIPATION OF WELCOMING THEM TO THE WORLD. WHAT A WONDERFUL THIRTEENTH BIRTHDAY GIFT THAT WOULD MAKE!

PRAYER

Thank You, God, for all my children. May I show them all the love they need to thrive.

PARENTING TEENS

THE TEEN YEARS INCLUDE INTENSE TRANSITIONS FOR THEM—AND US!

Adolescents are not monsters. They are just people
trying to learn how to make it among the adults in
the world, who are probably not so sure themselves.

VIRGINIA SATIR

 TO THINK ABOUT

- Do you have a "favorite age" for children when you just love being a parent? Is that age in the teen years?
- What are the struggles of being a teen today?
- What are the challenges of being a parent to teens today?

LESSON FOR LIFE

Promises

God will:

Give you wisdom
James 1:5

Love your teen—and
you—unconditionally
Romans 8:39

Protect and be
with your teen
Matthew 28:20

Guide your teen
John 17:17

What a Ride

BIBLE STUDY PASSAGE: LUKE 2:40-52

Jesus became wiser and grew physically. People liked him, and he pleased God.

LUKE 2:52

The teenage years are filled with changes and transitions—

- Physically, your teen must navigate the wonder—and sometimes strange and embarrassing moments—of puberty.
- Emotionally, your teen is often on a roller coaster ride due to physical and social changes.
- Socially, your teen is now looking to peers as much as adults for approval, which is always good for a few conflicts with parents.
- Spiritually, your teen must now begin to make matters of faith a personal decision and commitment, not just a matter of believing what Mom and Dad believe.

It would be great if we knew how Jesus' parents handled Him as a teen. All we know about Him from ages twelve to thirty is that He "increased in wisdom and stature and favor with God and man" (Luke 2:52 NKJV). Of course, Jesus' experience in the Temple at age twelve, when He worried His parents silly because He stayed behind to discuss theology with the teachers there, is a clue that as a real person, He too experienced transition and growth.

There are no secrets to parenting teens, but a few reminders include—

- Avoid bearing hard when there's conflict (Ephesians 6:4). The old cliché is still true: Attack problems, not people.
- Teach responsibility (Galatians 6:5). The happiest teens are those who have responsibilities. They are also the most prepared for the impending challenges of adulthood.
- Don't withdraw discipline, even if other parents seem to (Proverbs 29:17).
- Listen (James 1:19). Our kids will "hear" our words much more clearly when we listen to them.
- Enjoy them (Proverbs 23:24). Your teen will pick up on how you really feel about them, whether you say it aloud or not. That doesn't guarantee that they won't be difficult and distant anyway, but as the adult, you need to exhibit the maturity of a consistent love! ➤

> If you go the wrong way—to the right or to the left—you will hear a voice behind you saying, "This is the right way. You should go this way."
> Isaiah 30:21

REAL LIFE

It's All in the Attitude

CHARLENE FRIESEN

It's official: I am an embarrassment to my adolescent son. I need not utter a word because my mere presence is suffocating. Who knew it would be so easy, yet so hard?

Last January, my "tweenager" brought home an information form detailing a school ski day. He rolled his eyes as I filled out my chaperone and registration forms. Even better, we were enrolled in the same beginner's class. That's almost as good as tousling your son's hair in front of his friends.

Ski day finally arrived. We joined a class of ten-year-olds who spent most of their time either face up or face down. Chris and I were looking good in comparison. Our lesson went well—I learned the fine art of snowplowing as Chris learned how to avoid the big girl who insisted on calling him "son."

Before long, we were crisscrossing the bunny slopes with noodle-like legs. I shadowed Chris with backseat-skier commands: "Ice patch to your right, crying toddler to your left, tree dead ahead." As I approached him with one last word of motherly advice, a frosty stare and powdered peach fuzz moustache warned me to retreat.

I withdrew to the chairlift and spotted Chris. He had mastered the towrope but was still having trouble negotiating with his skis; they were doing the driving. He simply pointed his skis straight down and shot full speed to the bottom, just two stiff legs and two flailing arms heading straight for the nearest victim.

After getting up close and personal with a ski rack, he agreed to another lesson. Riding the chairlift, I instructed Chris, "When we exit from the chair, stay right and I'll stay out of your way." Visions of future driving lessons wafted through my head.

This lesson was scarier than driver training; there was no airbag to inflate upon impact. Chris, the non-conformist, ignored the instructor and promptly swished to the bottom of the hill. I'm still not sure if that was intentional or not. He left his airbag at the top of the hill to find her own way down.

I spent the rest of the day skiing solo and spying—those trees aren't just for looks, you know. Although I detested his hormonally charged, sassy attitude, I appreciated his attitude of perseverance and independence. Lesson or not, he was learning to ski from the ground up.

Chris blazed his own trails that day, and I know there will be many more to follow. Even though I may feel as welcome as a telephone solicitor, it is my God-given responsibility to help him pursue the right path so he can lead others on future trailblazing expeditions.

Armed with God's promise that His Word is a light for our path and motivated by the same gritty determination played out on the ski hill, I'm confident Chris will learn to navigate those slippery slopes of life. Ski rack and all. ➤

ACTION STEP

IT CAN BE A CHALLENGE TO FIND AS MANY COMMON ACTIVITIES ONCE YOUR CHILDREN HIT THEIR TEEN YEARS. IS THERE SOMETHING YOUR TEEN PARTICULARLY ENJOYS THAT YOU CAN ENJOY WITH HIM OR HER? YOU DON'T HAVE TO GO OUT AND BUY A SKATEBOARD AND ELBOW PADS (AND YOUR TEEN WOULD PROBABLY PREFER THAT YOU DIDN'T), BUT FIND A WAY THIS WEEK TO CONNECT WITH YOUR YOUNG ADULT.

PRAYER

God, grant me the patience, wisdom, grace, and joy I need to see my children through their teen years.

SELF-IMAGE

YOUR ABILITY TO LOVE OTHERS— INCLUDING YOUR CHILDREN—IS LINKED TO YOUR ABILITY TO LOVE YOURSELF.

The value of a person is not measured on an applause meter; it is measured in the heart and mind of God.

JOHN FISCHER

 To Think About

- What are some of the negative consequences of low self-esteem?
- What have been some of the determining factors in your ability to love yourself—or in your struggle to love yourself?
- How do you believe God views you? Do you accept His love?

LESSON FOR LIFE

Promises

God will:

Honor your kindness

Proverbs 19:22

Honor your inner beauty

1 Timothy 2:10

Proverbs 31:30

Accept you and
justify you

Romans 3:30

Love you as a mother
loves her baby

Isaiah 49:15

The Woman at the Well

BIBLE STUDY PASSAGE: 2 CORINTHIANS 5:1-10

*The Lord did not care for you and choose you because
there were many of you—you are the smallest nation of
all. But the Lord chose you because he loved you, and he
kept his promise to your ancestors.*

DEUTERONOMY 7:7-8

If ever there was a person who had reasons to struggle
with their self-image, it was the woman who met Jesus at the
well as recorded in John 4.

First of all, she was a Samaritan. In Jesus' day, the Jews
despised all Samaritans as religious infidels and "half breeds."
When Israel was conquered by the Babylonians in 586 B.C., the
youngest and most educated were taken into captivity. When
their descendants returned to Jerusalem seventy years later,
they expected to find a thriving center of worship and faith.
Instead, many who had been left behind converted to other
religions and married people from other countries. They were
despised from that moment on.

Second, she was a woman, which meant she had second-class status in her culture and was viewed as the "property" of her husband.

Third, she had failed at love. Jesus asked her where her husband was. She admitted she wasn't married, but was living with a man. Jesus pointed out she had previously been married five times! Whether a serial widow or divorcee, she had probably given up on marital vows.

Fourth, she was rejected by her peers. Jesus met her during the hottest time of the day with no one else around her. The women of Middle East villages gathered water at the well together during the coolest part of the day.

But when Jesus entered her life, everything changed. He took the initiative and spoke to her first, uncommon for a man to do in that culture. In the same way, He reaches out to us long before we reach toward Him. He looked at her as a person on the basis of her potential—not her past or even her present circumstances.

Most importantly, He offered her a living water that would satisfy the emptiness and longing of her soul, a drink of water that would provide renewal for her parched soul and life.

Even if you feel as needy as a lonely Samaritan at a well today, be assured that Jesus provides you with all the reasons you need to love and embrace yourself. ➡

So the King will greatly desire your beauty;
Because He is your Love, worship Him.
Psalm 45:11 NKJV

REAL LIFE

A Very Special Young Lady

NANCY B. GIBBS

During my childhood years, I had low self-esteem. Saying I wasn't fond of school is an understatement. Actually, I hated school. Every afternoon, I watched the clock waiting for the dismissal bell to ring. My grades reflected my low self-esteem—I had no desire to learn.

I had been a worrier my entire life. My father said many times that my first sentence was "I'm worried." For some reason, my intense worries kept me from being able to perform well in school or any other aspect of my life. As a result, I never saw myself as anyone worthwhile.

It seemed the older I got, the further behind I became. I was quiet, shy, and withdrawn. Very few people knew me. How could I expect anyone to understand me? I didn't even understand myself. I never felt like I did anything in an extraordinary way. I didn't have the desire to go to college—I didn't really have any interests I wanted to pursue.

I did have one ambition: When someone asked me what I wanted to become as an adult, my response was always, "A mother."

Little changed as I entered my teen years. I simply wanted to blend in with the crowd. I didn't want to be noticed. By the grace of God, I graduated from high school and married at an early age.

I was delighted when I discovered that I was expecting a child. I loved the thought of becoming a mother. Many of the students who attended high school with me were getting ready to go off to college. I was getting ready for what I anticipated would be the greatest day of my life.

God not only blessed me with one baby boy; He gave me two. Two nurses walked into my room the next morning, each holding a baby. I was too weak to hold both babies at one time, so one of the nurses stayed with me. I looked into my babies' tiny faces and rejoiced. I felt like I had done something right for the first time in my life.

In the quietness of the moment as I met my two little boys, the nurse smiled a warm and sensitive smile. "God must think you are a very special mother, honey, to have given you two babies at one time," she whispered.

"Who, me?" I inquired. "Special?"

"Yes, you," she said. "You must be a very special young lady." The nurse saw me as a special mother. God obviously saw me as His princess—a person worthy of His blessings.

To this day, some thirty-one years later, I remember how important I felt the day that God blessed me so richly. Even though I never saw myself as anyone special, God saw me as His child worthy of abundant blessings and His love. He made me a mother—and a very special mother indeed! ➤

ACTION STEP

YOU'VE WRITTEN LETTERS TO OTHERS AS A WAY TO AFFIRM YOUR LOVE FOR AND BELIEF IN THEM. WRITE A LETTER TO YOURSELF, REMINDING YOU OF HOW MUCH GOD LOVES YOU—AND YOUR OWN SENSE OF SELF-APPRECIATION. TUCK IT ANYWHERE YOU CAN READ IT AS A REMINDER OF THIS SOUL MATTER.

PRAYER

Thank You, God, for being the One who believes in me and loves me as no one else ever could. You see in my heart and declare me beautiful.

FEAR AND FAITH

THE ANTIDOTE TO A SUFFOCATING, STIFLING, STAGNATING FEAR IS SIMPLE FAITH.

Faith is not belief without proof,
but trust without reservations.

ELTON TRUEBLOOD

TO THINK ABOUT

- What is the difference between healthy concern and unhealthy fear?
- What role does faith play in your family life?
- Are there any areas in your life where you need more faith?

LESSON FOR LIFE

Promises

God will:

Bless you for believing
and trusting Him
John 20:29

Make you victorious
through faith
1 John 5:4

Be available to help you
Psalm 46:1-2
Deuteronomy 31:7-8

Free from Fear

BIBLE STUDY PASSAGE: PHILIPPIANS 4:4-7

So don't worry, because I am with you. Don't be afraid, because I am your God. I will make you strong and will help you; I will support you with my right hand that saves you.

ISAIAH 41:10

Nothing can rob you of joy, confidence, optimism, and opportunities more quickly than a spirit of fear.

Behavioral scientists have long debated whether the first emotion a baby experiences is love or fear. Because of the "startle reflex," many researchers believe it is the latter.

When we have children of our own, we experience all kinds of new fears—we fear for their future, their health, their safety.

There are many sources of fear. Some are unreasonable (to everyone else but the persons experiencing them!), and are considered unhealthy phobias. But whatever the source—a sense of the unknown, physical danger, spiritual warfare, financial crises, or reputation issues—fear is real and must be faced honestly.

One of the greatest promises of God is that we don't have to face our fears alone. He is always with us; never will He forsake us (Hebrews 13:5). In fact, when we truly experience His love, fear is cast away (1 John 4:18). Why? Love is what must be present for trust to flourish. So remember, if you fear—

Don't be afraid;
just believe.
Mark 5:36

- The past, God makes all things new (2 Corinthians 5:17);
- The future, God has promised you a future and a hope (Jeremiah 29:11);
- Enemies, God will protect and keep you (Deuteronomy 31:6);
- Financial problems, God will provide for your every need (Philippians 4:19);
- Death and dying, God has conquered the power of death and promises eternal life (Romans 8:1-2).

Are you ready to walk boldly, with a new sense of confidence today? Take a few steps toward God today and let Him handle the anxieties that trouble you. ➤➤

REAL LIFE

Faith is the Key

PEGGY FREZON

I stared at the flimsy wooden door of my eighteen-year-old daughter's off-campus apartment and gulped. Something was wrong. There was a big, gaping hole inside the metal ring where the lock should be.

I grabbed her arm. "No lock? Kate, there might as well be a big flashing neon sign with the words, 'Unsupervised girls! Free laptops! Step inside!'"

Kate tried to calm me; she surely felt I was overprotective. "Mom, don't worry, it'll be fine. My door has a lock."

True enough—her actual apartment door inside the house required a key, as did the five other apartments. But the actual door—the main entry for the whole house—would be open, offering free access to anyone who happened by.

Looking around the front hall, my imagination ran wild. I envisioned intruders hiding in the corner, hidden by the dark walnut woodwork. I pictured shady characters in the shadowy stairwell, even inside the antique hinged wooden bench by the door. But what could I do? I felt awful when it came time to leave her there.

Later, at home 200 miles away, I couldn't stop worrying. Kate was a responsible college student, but things happened. I tossed and turned all night wondering if she was safe. The next morning, weary-eyed, I decided to call her landlord. "Did you know there's no lock on the apartment house door?"

There was a slight hesitation, then a little laugh. "I'm sorry, Mrs. Frezon," he replied. "I had one there, but the kids kept locking themselves out." I was about to respond with heartfelt pleas, but he went on. "Even if I did install a new lock, the kids won't use it." He explained that, in the past, the students would repeatedly defeat the lock. I sighed. A new lock would be pretty much as useful as the gaping hole that existed there already.

What could I do now? Educate the other occupants about crime statistics? Force Kate to abandon her friends and move to a dorm? Drag her home? The point had come when I could do nothing, absolutely nothing. I worried. I checked in with her frequently to make sure she was still alive. I worried some more.

Then one day I was walking through the store and I saw a little trinket. It was shaped like a house key, inscribed with the words, "Faith is the key." My mind immediately raced to the lock—or lack of lock—on my daughter's door. And then I thought about that one little word: faith. Had I forgotten?

Of course, faith was the only real solution to my anxiety. Right then and there I gave the situation to God. "I trust You, Lord, to keep my daughter safe." I knew there was no way I could protect Kate. But God could. I felt surrounded by a warm, comforting feeling. I couldn't lock Kate's doors at night, but I didn't need to when God was standing guard. ➤

ACTION STEP

BRENDAN FRANCIS SAYS, "MANY OF OUR FEARS ARE TISSUE-PAPER-THIN, AND A SINGLE COURAGEOUS STEP WOULD CARRY US CLEAR THROUGH THEM."

WHAT IS ONE FEAR YOU ARE LIVING WITH TODAY—AND WHAT IS ONE STEP YOU CAN TAKE TO BREAK THROUGH IT? DETERMINE A STEP THAT YOU CAN CARRY OUT WITHIN THE NEXT FORTY-EIGHT HOURS.

PRAYER

Your love, Heavenly Father, is ever been present in my life and I will always cling to Your love with faith and trust when I feel fear and anxiety in my life. Thank You for always being close.

STRAINED RELATIONSHIPS

SOME RELATIONSHIPS, EVEN WITH OUR OWN KIDS, ARE DIFFICULT AND DEMANDING AND REQUIRE SPECIAL HANDLING.

*If you have never been hated by your child,
you have never been a parent.*

BETTE DAVIS

 TO THINK ABOUT

- Do you have one or more relationships that seem to be in a constant state of turmoil and strain? How does it make you feel?
- Have you ever sat down and identified your contributions to the stress and strain?
- Do you ever take blame and responsibility for dynamics that are not of your own doing and that you can't control?

LESSON FOR LIFE

Promises

God will:

Give you happiness for
being a peacemaker
Matthew 5:9

Reward your persistence
Galatians 6:9

Reward your discipline
Proverbs 29:15

Give you patience
Galatians 5:22

Take Heart

BIBLE STUDY PASSAGE: GENESIS 33:1-15

Love is patient and kind. Love is not jealous, it does not brag, and it is not proud. Love is not rude, is not selfish, and does not get upset with others. Love does not count up wrongs that have been done.

1 CORINTHIANS 13:4-5

If you are living with guilt due to an unrealistic expectation that you should—and that you can—get along with everyone in your life, take heart and give yourself a break.

Even our Lord, Jesus Christ, experienced conflict with His family. On one occasion, His parents took Him to the Passover celebration at the Temple in Jerusalem. Because they were traveling with a large group of friends and family members, it was the next day before they realized they'd left Him behind. After being scolded by His parents, Jesus' curt response was: "Didn't you know that I must be in my Father's house?" (Luke 2:49).

As an adult in His thirties, on the road as a vagabond preacher, Jesus worried His mother and brothers so much that they went to take Him home because they thought He'd gone crazy (Mark 3:21).

David had deep conflicts with his oldest son, Absalom, who tried to wrest the throne from his father (see 2 Samuel 15). Joseph was despised by his brothers and sold into slavery by them (Genesis 37:28). It was only after a twenty-year separation that Jacob and Esau were reunited in forgiveness and love (Genesis 33:4). Paul constantly implored his churches: "Make me very happy by having the same thoughts, sharing the same love, and having one mind and purpose" (Philippians 2:2).

If conflict is inevitable in some relationship—and sometimes that seems to be the case, no matter how much you love and how hard you try—what can you do?

- Do your best to keep peace—but don't live in guilt if it's not reciprocated (Romans 12:18).
- Exhibit patience and realize it takes a lot longer for some people, yes, even your own kids, to find their way (Ephesians 4:2).
- Persevere—one of the ways love takes hold is by being consistent and faithful (1 Corinthians 13:7, Galatians 6:9).
- Pray persistently for reconciliation and peace (Ephesians 6:18). ➤

Make your father and mother happy; give your mother a reason to be glad.

Proverbs 23:25

REAL LIFE

A Love Letter from a Porcupine

TEENA M. STEWART

My friend Debbie explained the hurt inflicted by her angry teenage daughter. Our accounts were similar. We could have swapped daughters and no one would have noticed. I wanted to assure her that things would turn out okay, but remembered the nightmare of being locked into that Doctor Jekyll and Ms. Hyde relationship with my own teen.

My oldest daughter and I love the same types of movies, books, and crafts. As much as I have always wanted to have that close relationship with my other daughter, it has often been like trying to love a porcupine. Whenever I try to get close, her quills prick me. Occasionally we make a good connection, but such moments are rare.

I wanted to tell my friend that there is hope. My daughter's rough edges have softened over time—I have caught glimpses of a softer heart with increasing frequency. Still, I struggle with the clumsy relationship. With empty nest years at hand, my oldest child is already on her own. My second oldest daughter is finishing up college and still living at home. We are still often like strangers passing on the street.

This year, my son graduates high school. The impending freedom should elate me, but instead I mourn my lost youth. Should-haves and could-haves make their way into my thoughts—if only I had done things differently, then maybe my kids would have a stronger faith and my daughter and I a closer relationship.

One morning I walked into my home office ready to start work. On my computer keyboard was a folded note with the word "Mom" on the outside. A rush of fear weakened me. Now what had I done to upset her? I began reading.

> *Mom,*
>
> *I've been doing a lot of thinking and only now do I realize how much I've taken you for granted. You are a great mother. You have stuck with me through so much. You're the person I talk to when Lee [her boyfriend] is making me crazy. I like chatting with you in the morning before I leave for work. It makes me feel like I'm beginning to make up for all those years of teenage angst I put you and Dad through. I know there were times you wanted to wring my neck. I can't blame you. But without you two, I would have failed high school or something worse. Thanks for not giving up...*

She went on to tell me that she loved our shared appreciation for art. No one else in our family connected that way. It was our special bond. She artfully signed the letter with "the loud one" in parentheses.

I smiled. I love this tough, loud, even sometimes belligerent child. Underneath those prickly quills is a tender heart. Had she sensed my feelings?

I couldn't wait to share this piece of hope with my friend. In a few more years, maybe her daughter will write her letters too. "See, Debbie," I wanted to say, "You're not doing such a bad job after all." →

ACTION STEP

SOME RELATIONSHIPS ARE "PRICKLY" ENOUGH THAT EVEN THE MOST SIMPLE OF CONVERSATIONS BECOME CONTESTS OF WILLS! IF YOU HAVE A STRAINED RELATIONSHIP WITH ONE OF YOUR CHILDREN—OR SOMEONE ELSE IMPORTANT IN YOUR LIFE—WRITE A HANDWRITTEN NOTE AFFIRMING YOUR LOVE AND APPRECIATION. THIS MIGHT BE A GOOD PRACTICE TO AVOID PETTY ARGUMENTS.

PRAYER

Lord God, make me a peacemaker, not a pot-stirrer. Please help me spread Your love and peace around me.

TOUGH TIMES

EVEN IN THE MIDST OF ADVERSITY, GOD IS PRESENT AND AT WORK IN OUR LIVES.

Snuggle in God's arms. When you are hurting, when you feel lonely, left out, let Him cradle you, comfort you, reassure you of His all-sufficient power and love.

KAY ARTHUR

TO THINK ABOUT

- Have you ever felt forgotten by God? Like He wasn't really working in your life?
- What situation are you praying about today?
- How have you seen God help you during difficult times?

LESSON FOR LIFE

Promises

God Will:

Give you strength
for each day
Philippians 4:13

Comfort you when
life is tough
2 Corinthians 1:4

Give you hope
for the future
Jeremiah 29:11

Send angels to
watch over you
Psalm 91:11

When the Going Gets Tough

BIBLE STUDY PASSAGE: 2 CORINTHIANS 12:7-10

God is our protection and our strength. He always helps in times of trouble.

PSALM 46:1

One of the greatest heroes of faith is the Apostle Paul. Churches, hospitals, schools, and even cities are named after him to honor his great contributions to the Church of Jesus Christ. He wrote thirteen letters in the New Testament, and almost half of the book of Acts (chapters 9 and 13-28) is written about his life.

You might think that a man who was that powerful probably had everything go his way. But that is not the case. He had an incredibly tough life. In fact, one Roman historian described him as a short, red-headed, ugly man (Josephus).

Some of the trials that happened to him were—

- He was shipwrecked (Acts 27:13-28:10).
- He was attacked by a mob who didn't like his teaching and left for dead (Acts 21:30-32).

- He was imprisoned for being a Christian (Acts 16:23).
- He was criticized by church people who preferred other leaders (2 Corinthians 10:10, 12:11).
- He even had physical problems (Galatians 4:13).

Despite all these incredible difficulties, Paul was joyful (Philippians 2:29), and he trusted God to take care of him and make him a conqueror (Philippians 4:13).

When life is tough, our souls get discouraged. Don't give up and lose faith. You can trust God! ⇒

But those who have troubles will not be forgotten. The hopes of the poor will never die.
Psalm 9:18

REAL LIFE

He Touched Me

CAROL HILLEBRENNER

On that cold, gray, February morning as I tromped through snow to the chicken coop, God seemed gone from my life. My husband's business was faltering, our seventeen-year-old son was in coronary care with a viral inflammation of his heart, my father-in-law was in the next room with a heart attack, our fifteen-year-old daughter was threatening to get pregnant so she could get her own apartment, and our youngest child, who was doing everything right, was feeling ignored.

The single light bulb in the coop flickered and died, so I shivered in the gloom as I scattered grain for the chickens in their fenced portion of the shed and dipped dry food from a bucket for the dozen or so barn cats strapping my ankles. As I thawed frozen watering pans with hot water, a sparrow dropped down from a low rafter to grab a piece of corn from the floor of the chickens' pen. The cats stopped crunching cat food at sight of a hot meal on the wing, poured down the ladder from their feeding shelf, and climbed the fence or dodged through the open gate. The sparrow barely took off before the first cat reached it and flew around inside the shadowy chicken coop, bumping into rafters as cats leaped and climbed after it.

Suddenly a shaft of sunlight fell through the slightly open doorway. The sparrow flew into the golden trail of light and fluttered off with his bit of corn.

Slogging through snow on the way back to the house, I remembered the biblical statement that God knew even when a sparrow fell from heaven. Suddenly furious, I threw down my water pails, looked up at that grim gray sky, and shouted, "What about me, God? You saved that sparrow, but what about me?"

Nothing happened, as I expected. God obviously had better things to do—like save sparrows.

Sighing with frustration, I bent to pick up my pails and felt a touch like a warm caress on my cold, bare left hand. Looking down, I was amazed to see a golden shaft of sunlight warming my skin. Before I could look up for the break in the clouds, the sunbeam was gone. As I stood up holding my buckets, I realized I felt just like that sparrow must have when it saw a shaft of light in the dark coop. Life no longer seemed so dark and hopeless.

A few days later, my husband was called in on a big contracting job, my son and father-in-law came home within a week, and I was able to spend more time with my younger daughter. My fifteen-year-old still drives us crazy on a regular basis—but life without a few challenges might allow me to forget how thankful I am to God. →

ACTION STEP

PLANTS, FLOWERS, TREES, AND OTHER VEGETATION LAY DORMANT IN DARK SOIL FOR A SEASON, ONLY TO MIRACULOUSLY BREAK FORTH IN LIFE. HOPE IS THE SAME WAY.

STOP BY A NURSERY AND PURCHASE A SEED PACKET OR SMALL PLANT OF A FLOWER OR VEGETABLE YOU LOVE. PLANT THE SEED AND CARE FOR IT. KEEP THE POT ON A WINDOWSILL YOU PASS OFTEN AS A BRIGHT REMINDER THAT NO MATTER WHAT YOU'RE FACING, HOPE IS NEVER LOST.

PRAYER

Father God, You know the things I'm facing today that threaten to suffocate my hope. But thank You that You give me the strength I need each minute of each day.

KIDS AND THEIR CHOICES

OUR FAITH IS A BLESSING TO OUR CHILDREN'S SPIRITUAL GROWTH, BUT THEY ARE ULTIMATELY RESPONSIBLE FOR THEIR CHOICES AND THEIR OWN FAITH IN GOD.

The hardest part of raising a child is teaching them to ride bicycles.
A shaky child on a bicycle for the first time needs both support and freedom.
The realization that this is what the child will always need can hit hard.

SLOAN WILSON

 To Think About

- Why is it so hard to let children make their own decisions?
- What are some of the things we can learn about parenting from how God deals with us?
- What are the hallmarks of loving discipline?

LESSON FOR LIFE

Promises

God will:

Hear your prayers

Psalm 18:6

Bless your children

Psalm 112:2

Calm your anxieties

Philippians 4:7

Choose This Day

BIBLE STUDY PASSAGE: DEUTERONOMY 11

Instead, each person will die for his own sin; the person who eats sour grapes will grind his own teeth.

JEREMIAH 31:29-30

When Joshua declared, "As for me and my family, we will serve the Lord" (Joshua 24:15), he reinforced the important Old Testament concept of "generational blessings and curses." He framed this in the form of a negative warning: "If you leave the Lord and serve other gods, he will send you great trouble" (24:20). Other biblical thinkers expressed the positive corollary of this: "But the Lord's love for those who respect him continues forever and ever, and his goodness continues to their grandchildren" (Psalm 103:17).

Later in the Old Testament, the concept of personal responsibility begins to emerge. Ezekiel says: "A child will not be punished for a parent's sin, and a parent will not be punished for a child's sin." (18:20).

There are two realities that all of us as parents must understand:

- The way we love and live for God makes a huge impact on our children's spiritual receptivity.
- Ultimately, all of us are responsible to respond to God in faith.

There is freedom from guilt and even anger when we fully accept that second reality. Too many of us, disappointed with our kids' choices, get caught in a spiral of negative parenting that starts with guilt, transitions to force and manipulation, and sometimes sinks to a withholding of love. And it's true that we can control behavior to a degree through such methods. But we can also lose our kids' hearts.

Our job is to love our kids unconditionally, teach them right from wrong, and help them accept responsibility for their own lives. From there, they truly are responsible for their choices—even their bad ones. In today's culture, our temptation is to overprotect our kids from the consequences of their choices. Small wonder children are living with their parents into their thirties, with no intentions of moving out!

Just as Joshua's challenge to "choose this day" is a call to faith you must settle in your heart, so it is a call your children must answer to.

Are you willing to love them so much that you let them choose for themselves? ➡

Train up a child in the way he should go, And when he is old he will not depart from it.
Proverbs 22:6 NKJV

REAL LIFE

Coming Home

KEITH KILBY

I could tell by my mother's voice that she wanted me home for Christmas. It felt good knowing that despite my past mistakes, I was still welcome.

As the plane made its descent into the Houston airport, I began to wonder if my mother would even recognize me. I had gone through so many changes. As I waited at the passenger pick-up area, I heard that familiar voice calling my name. In moments, I was back in her arms. It felt so good to hug her as hard as I could. I didn't want to let her go.

There was so much to catch up on after five years. Would the rest of the family be as welcoming? As we pulled into the driveway of my parents' home, I felt the old adage "home sweet home" ring true. How grateful I was that the love in our family had held steady as my dad and the rest of the family enthusiastically welcomed me.

I knew I wasn't what you would call an ideal son. My parents took me to church and taught me how to live a good life, but as a teen, I explored avenues other than what I had been taught at home. Instead of pursuing my other artistic talents, my heart was set on singing in a hard metal band. It offered a life of sex, drugs, and rock and roll that was too hard for me to resist and eventually landed me in jail over and over.

I couldn't understand why my family wouldn't help with my ensuing legal problems. They kept in close contact and prayed for me, but I felt that they were being stubborn and selfish by not bailing me out. I know now that it was the hardest thing in the world for them to show me tough love and make me face the consequences of my actions. It was me who was being selfish.

Now I was a free man—not just released from jail, but released from my old way of life. In prison, I began to understand the sacrifice that Jesus made for me on the cross, dying on my behalf. It was as though a veil had been lifted from my eyes allowing me to see the love and grace of God that had been there all along. Now, I wanted to become a blessing to others, especially my family.

This Christmas, I planned to tell my parents that I didn't want to just come home for the holidays, that like the prodigal son, I was ready to return to my relationship with God. Over the years, their prayers had carried me, and I slowly became aware of what I had been taught as a child and began to thank God for such a loving mother and father.

It was good to be back home—back to their loving arms and the loving arms of my Heavenly Father. →

ACTION STEP

THINK ABOUT THE MOST IMPORTANT DECISIONS IN YOUR CHILDREN'S LIFE—
WHO THEY MARRY, WHAT THEY DO AFTER HIGH SCHOOL, WHAT KINDS OF
FRIENDS THEY CHOOSE, AND WHAT THEY BELIEVE. TAKE TIME EACH DAY THIS
WEEK TO PRAY FOR THESE AREAS, ASKING GOD TO REMOVE FROM YOUR HEART
ANY FEELINGS OF FEAR OR RESENTMENT.

PRAYER

God, I know that You've been patient with me. Thank You for loving me. Help me give my children the loving discipline that You've given me.

SEEKING FORGIVENESS

GOD DOES NOT WANT US TO CARRY
A LOAD OF GUILT ON OUR BACKS, BUT TO
ACCEPT HIS FORGIVENESS AND MOVE ON.

*In some families, please is described as the
magic word. In our house, however, it was sorry.*

MARGARET LAURENCE

 TO THINK ABOUT

- Are you carrying around a sense of guilt today?
- How does not forgiving ourselves or seeking forgiveness from others thwart God's plans for our lives?
- Is there someone in your life you need to forgive so they can move on?

LESSON FOR LIFE

Promises

God's Amazing Mercy

BIBLE STUDY PASSAGE: PSALM 51

God will:

Heal and restore
Isaiah 61:3, 57:18

God, be merciful to me because you are loving. Because you are always ready to be merciful, wipe out all my wrongs. Wash away all my guilt and make me clean again.

PSALM 51:1-2

Forgive you
Acts 10:43

Cleanse you
1 John 1:8-9

Forget your sins
Micah 7:19

You don't understand some of the things I've done. I'm not sure God can—or would even want to—forgive me. And even if He could, I don't think I can forgive myself.

Even the great heroes of the Bible had serious character flaws and were in need of God's mercy!

Jacob, the son of Isaac and one of the fathers of our faith, tricked his twin brother and even his beloved father, in order to "steal" the family birthright (Genesis 25-27).

Moses, who led the Hebrew slaves from the Pharaoh's oppression in Egypt, murdered a man and lived as a fugitive for forty years (Exodus 2-3).

David, perhaps the most beloved and popular of Israel's kings throughout history, performed many acts of courage, faith, and mercy—slaying the giant, Goliath, and sparing King

Saul, a sworn enemy to him, to name just two—but also had a litany of sins and shortcomings strewn along his past.

His greatest crime was what he did to Uriah the Hittite, one of his bravest and most loyal soldiers. David coveted and then "took" Uriah's wife, Bathsheba, to be his own. To make his evil act even worse, he had Uriah killed to try and cover up what he had done. (See 2 Samuel 11-12 for the whole story.)

Throughout the Psalms, and especially in Psalm 51, David cries out for God's mercy. He knows that being the king doesn't get him off the hook. He knows that no act of contrition can undo his evil deeds.

There is no sin so great that God's grace is not greater. You may be carrying around guilt of words spoken in anger at your kids or in jealousy of a friend. But be assured that God's mercy can and will unburden your heart and make it pure again. ➤

And he will turn
The hearts of the fathers
to the children,
And the hearts of the
children to their fathers.
Malachi 4:6 NKJV

REAL LIFE

Slow Boil

SUSIE HAMILTON

I had been building to a slow boil. No one seemed to be helping me around the house, including my husband. He said that if I simply stated my needs clearly instead of nagging, he and the kids would respond better and help more. Sigh. That's what I had been doing for two months, but I sure didn't see any additional help.

One of my biggest pet peeves is what turned my slow boil into a torrent of steam.

There had been some theft in our neighborhood, and several expensive items had been taken from our open garage in broad daylight. I had been beating the drum that we needed to keep the door shut, especially with my twelve-year-old son, who tends not to pay attention.

One Saturday, when I pulled into the driveway after running an errand, the garage door was wide open with no one around. Tears of anger clouded my eyes. I took the groceries in and began putting them away.

When Justin bounced into the house, not a care in the world, I went off. His eyes were wide with wonder and fear as for the first time in his life he heard his sweet, patient mother rant and rave. To my own horror, I heard myself hurling a few cuss words into the air.

"But, Mom," he said, adding extra syllables to "MOM."

"No way. I've had enough 'mom!' I want some cooperation. And I mean now. I also want your cell phone and your scooter. I'm keeping them until you get on the stick. Now go to your room!"

He glumly handed me his phone and thumped down the hall. I was still seething.

You can imagine my shock when I heard some hammering coming from the garage. I opened the door and saw my smiling husband working on a shelving unit to organize our tools and toys.

"Where's Justin?" he asked. "He's helping me put this stuff together. I go in the back yard and the kid disappears on me," he said with mock sarcasm.

"What's wrong?" he asked after seeing the horrified expression on my face.

Apparently the guys had gone to the back yard to mix some stain. When I got home, I didn't realize they were at the house working.

What do you do when you've blown it? Really messed up? My first thought was to defend myself. After all, I wasn't wrong that some of my family members weren't pulling their weight. And my interpretation of the open garage door was reasonable. Cussing at my son might be another matter...

I apologized. I asked for forgiveness. I got a half-hearted hug from Justin in response. We later had a long family powwow that got a lot of issues on the table.

I discovered that Justin's forgiveness of me was not immediate and automatic. I also discovered that my forgiveness of him and my husband wasn't quite as simple as words, either.

The greatest lesson I learned was that giving and receiving forgiveness opened my heart to God's grace and mercy. As we forgave, He softened my heart and made it possible for us to lovingly work on our relationship. ➤

ACTION STEP

IF THERE ARE PAST SINS THAT HAVE HAUNTED YOU—AND YOU HAVE TRULY ASKED GOD'S FORGIVENESS—THEN IT IS TIME TO MOVE ON. MAYBE A SYMBOLIC ACT WILL HELP MAKE FORGIVENESS MORE REAL TO YOU. WRITE DOWN THAT THING—OR THOSE THINGS—ON A SHEET OF PAPER. SAY A SHORT PRAYER, AND THEN LIGHT THE PAPER ON FIRE AND LET THAT SYMBOLIZE GOD'S ACT OF SCATTERING YOUR SINS AS FAR AS THE EAST IS FROM THE WEST.

PRAYER

Heavenly Father, thank You for saving my soul, forgiving me of my sins, and giving me a new life in You.

DIFFICULT KIDS

ALL CHILDREN ARE A BLESSING FROM GOD—EVEN THOSE WHO REQUIRE SPECIAL HANDLING.

A child is a handful some of the time,
but a heartful all of the time.

ANONYMOUS

TO THINK ABOUT

- What are the challenges you face in raising your children?
- What are your children's special needs?
- How do difficult kids affect the climate of a family?

LESSON FOR LIFE

Promises

God will:

Produce patience
in your life
Galatians 5:22

Give you loving discipline
Proverbs 3:12

Bless you and your
children when
you obey Him
Deuteronomy 12:28

Your Special Child

BIBLE STUDY PASSAGE: PROVERBS 3:1-12

*Train children how to live right, and when they are old,
they will not change.*

PROVERBS 22:6

Difficult behavior in children can take many forms, from aggression and defiance to clinginess and stubbornness to loudness and hyperactivity to just plain whining.

So are children difficult because they deliberately want to cause pain? Are they difficult because of bad parenting?

The reality seems to be that some children are simply born with a more difficult temperament. They are harder to raise. They can make us feel angry and inadequate, exhausted and bewildered, even embarrassed and isolated. They can create a strain on all family relationships, including marriage.

Is there hope? Absolutely! Stubborn, defiant children can become positive, energetic, and creative teens and young adults, but require some extra parental "management."

There is no simple approach to dealing with difficult children, because their problematic behaviors are very different

and there are many age issues. But a few useful suggestions
from experts include—

- Define problem behaviors. Expectations, rules, and
  boundaries need to be reinforced more often with
  difficult children.
- Get out of the emotional blame game. If your child, who
  has more difficulty understanding his or her behavior, is
  constantly told he or she is bad, their self-esteem and
  family connection will suffer. Likewise, when you beat
  yourself up for what you could or should do better, you
  are unable to deal with problems in a healthy way.
- Add extra structure to your home life and interact with
  children in a way that heads off many problems before
  they start. Part of the structure that difficult children
  need is interaction with caring parents.
- Get the help of others. Don't be embarrassed to visit a
  counselor to help you and your family better manage.
  Ask a few trusted friends to pray with you.
- Seek God's help. "Trust the Lord with all your heart, and
  don't depend on your own understanding. Remember
  the Lord in all you do, and he will give you success"
  (Proverbs 3:5-6). Prayer makes a difference! ➤

If you love your children,
you will correct them.
Proverbs 13:24

REAL LIFE

My Precious Boy

CATHI LUNDY

We were blessed with one of those "difficult" children. Our second child, a son, came after an "easy" daughter. Now we never ask if someone has a "good" baby. All babies are good. Some are just easier than others. For our second child, life always seemed harder. He started ten days late—I think he never would have left the womb without inducement.

We endured months of colic, trying every remedy. My husband walked him outside in the middle of the night, singing and pointing out stars. Our brave babysitters would leave wheel marks in the hardwood floors from rocking the whole crib to calm him down.

And of course, as a toddler he had tantrums. Loud noises startled him, large groups made him nervous—he would "hit the wall," as we'd say, and have meltdowns. He hated to go anywhere, even fun places.

"Let's go to the park," I'd say cheerfully, hoping. And he would cry, "No, no, no...."

So I'd scoop him up, strap him in his seat, and take him crying to the park or the beach or wherever else he didn't want to go. Once there, he'd have a great time. I learned to laugh and pick him up and carry him along with our life even if he didn't think he wanted to go along with the program.

But some days I worried: *Will he be okay? Am I doing something wrong? If he's this hard now, what will he be like as a teenager?*

One afternoon as he cried in his bed, I cried in our bathroom. Those questions rang in my head. And it came to me that my son needed to feel faith coming from his mother, not fear about his future.

I started simply by speaking my new belief out loud. I called him "my precious boy." I spoke it while we played, bathed, and dressed to affirm that he was precious and lovable to me.

A few months later, I attended a mothers group at a nearby church. While we shared our burdens and prayed, the kids played across the hall. One unforgettable day, he came out with his first drawing, one of a little boy smiling. He presented it to me and said, "Mommy, here is a happy face of your precious boy."

Emotions welled up inside me—gratefulness that God is faithful; amazement that my child saw himself as happy; joy that he knew he was my precious boy.

That day still carries me through as we tread those dreaded teenage years. He didn't stop being difficult that day. But he showed me how much my words shaped his self-concept, that God was faithful, and that my son knew he would always be my precious boy. ➸

ACTION STEP

DO YOU HAVE A DIFFICULT CHILD? HERE ARE A FEW DIAGNOSTIC QUESTIONS. RATE YOUR CHILD IN EACH OF THE FOLLOWING AREAS ON A SCALE OF ZERO TO FIVE, ZERO BEING NO PROBLEM, FIVE BEING AN EXTREME PROBLEM.

- DO YOU FEEL THAT YOUR CHILD IS HARD TO RAISE?
- DO YOU HAVE TROUBLE UNDERSTANDING YOUR CHILD'S BEHAVIOR?
- DO YOU OFTEN FIND YOURSELF LOCKED IN A BATTLE OF WILLS OR ARGUING?
- DO YOU OFTEN EXPERIENCE FEELINGS OF GUILT OR INADEQUACY AS A PARENT?
- DOES YOUR CHILD'S BEHAVIOR AFFECT YOUR MARRIAGE AND THE OVERALL ATMOSPHERE IN YOUR HOUSE?

DO YOU HAVE ENOUGH PARENTING TOOLS TO WORK WITH A DIFFICULT CHILD? WHERE WILL YOU TURN TO GROW?

PRAYER

God, all Your children are wonderful. Please give me patience and wisdom today.

RECONCILIATION

WITH GOD'S GRACE,
EVEN THE MOST DAMAGED
RELATIONSHIPS CAN BE RESTORED.

*Extend a hand whether or not
you know it shall be grasped.*

RYUNOSUKE SATORO

 ## TO THINK ABOUT

- Is there someone in your life from whom you are estranged?
- What is the hardest part of healing a broken relationship?
- Are there some relationships that can never be restored?

LESSON FOR LIFE

Promises

God will:

See that love prevails

1 Peter 4:8

Heal and restore

Isaiah 61:3

Make you a minister
of reconciliation

2 Corinthians 5:18

Remove your sorrows

Zephaniah 3:18

Messengers of Peace

BIBLE STUDY PASSAGE: EPHESIANS 2:14-22

*In Christ, there is no difference between Jew and Greek,
slave and free person, male and female. You are all the
same in Christ Jesus.*

GALATIANS 3:28

Jesus tells His disciples: "If you forgive anyone his sins,
they are forgiven. If you don't forgive them, they are not
forgiven" (John 20:23). In the Lord's Prayer, He teaches us:
"Forgive us for our sins, just as we have forgiven those who
sinned against us" (Matthew 6:12).

One of the most important soul matters in God's eyes is
reconciliation. Just as He sent His Son Jesus into the world to
reconcile people to Him (Colossians 1:20-22), so He tells us to
be reconciled even to our enemies (Matthew 5:44).

*But my husband left me. My friend betrayed me. I've just
never gotten along with my own parents.*

Obviously, one person cannot control or force the process
of reconciliation. That's why we are told to keep peace "as
much as depends on you" (Romans 12:18 NKJV). But before

216

ignoring the call to reconciliation as too hard, too painful, and very unrealistic, we need to remember—

- Reconciliation is God's idea and His way of doing things (Romans 5:8-10).
- Reconciliation is tied to our worship of God—He wants us to come before Him with right relationships (Matthew 5:23).
- As we forgive others, we are forgiven by God (Luke 6:37).

A few notes of caution on this topic include:

- Reconciliation does not always happen all at once, but can take place over years, so don't get discouraged or give up by lack of results (Galatians 6:9).
- Reconciliation does not mean we submit ourselves to abuse and cruelty by others. Even Jesus told His disciples to avoid certain people (Matthew 10:14).
- Due to past sins, sometimes relationships are simply changed forever. Someone who has left a spouse and family may seek and receive forgiveness, but be unable to resume their role in the lives of those they left.

Who can you draw close to today? A parent? A child? ➡

And above all things have fervent love for one another, for "love will cover a multitude of sins."
1 Peter 4:8 NKJV

REAL LIFE

A Wreath and a Cup of Tea

MARGARET LANG

"Oh, for the things I might have said, the things I might have done." My eyes were riveted to the inscription beneath the oil painting. Unlike the airy Impressionist paintings we had just viewed, this piece depicted a somber funeral wreath on a glossy black door.

On the subway ride home, I thought about Mom. How close she sat beside me, yet how distant. There were many things I could have done with Mom over the years, but I didn't.

Vignettes of my past appeared before my eyes. I saw Mom seated quietly at the table after another of her delicious home-cooked dinners while I giggled on Dad's lap. I saw Dad and me working diligently on a puzzle while Mom labored over dishes. At a party, my gregarious dad and I laughed arm-in-arm, while quieter Mom was who knows where.

The subway jolted to a stop, and with it my former ways. From then on, things would be different. Home from college, I would try to show Mom how much she meant to me.

That night, I gave Mom the hug usually reserved for Dad. She stood stiff, unsure of how to respond.

What can I do to reach her with my love? I asked the Lord. In a flash it occurred to me. Her British heritage was the key—maybe we could connect over her love of all things English.

"Mom, could we have a cup of tea together this afternoon?" I asked the next day.

Startled, she replied, "Why yes...of course, dear."

She carefully laid out her best china with a silver teapot, a pitcher of cream, a bowl of sugar, even a plate of shortbread—my favorite. At first we held our cups and saucers rigidly, but our fingers relaxed their grip as our hearts began to open up.

As we made tea time a regular institution, formal talk became easy chatter. Mom gave it a name, "girlie gab," and each day the intricate threads of our lives wove themselves tighter in a meaningful relationship.

That summer, we sat side-by-side in an oil painting class. We read and discussed novels, including the one Mom had written. And we potted chrysanthemums, anticipating the coming fall and my return to college.

In years later, my marriage took me miles away—until the autumn of her life. When Dad passed on and she suffered a mild stroke, I brought her back East with me.

That was the year to delight her with the laughter of children and lilacs and family photos, all while sipping a cup of English tea—together.

Then it was over.

She had to return to the Midwest, and I steeled myself for the looming finality of her trip. The book of "the things I might have said and the things I might have done," was closing. There was nothing more I could do. ➤

"Goodbye, precious Mom," I said at the airport through tears. Her smile of thanks was all I needed.

Another summer came and went before I laid a wreath at her gravesite. How different it was from the cold wreath in that painting years ago. This one was personal, woven intricately with bright memories. I was thankful to have heeded the plea of the heavenly Artist to love before the hour had passed. And that made all the difference.

ACTION STEP

WHO IS SOMEONE FROM WHOM YOU ARE SEPARATED DUE TO A MAJOR OR MINOR GRIEVANCE, OR JUST DRIFTING APART? HOW SERIOUS IS THE CAUSE OF THE SEPARATION? WHAT MAKES IT HARDEST FOR YOU TO SEEK RAPPROCHEMENT? WHAT IS ONE SMALL STEP YOU CAN TAKE TODAY? ARE YOU READY?

PRAYER

Thank You, O God, that when I was far away from You and lost, You ventured to seek me out. Grant me the courage to draw close to the people in my life.

SINGLE MOMS

GOD PROVIDES EACH OF US EVERYTHING WE NEED TO SURVIVE—AND THRIVE.

I need a God who is with us always, everywhere, in the deepest depths as well as the highest heights. It is when things go wrong, when good things do not happen, when our prayers seem to have been lost, that God is most present. We do not need the sheltering wings when things go smoothly. We are closest to God in the darkness, stumbling along blindly.

MADELEINE L'ENGLE

TO THINK ABOUT

- What are some of the unique challenges of being a single mom?
- What are some of the challenges for a child who is in a single-parent family?
- What are some of the ways God has cared for you as a single mom?

LESSON FOR LIFE

Promises

God will:

Meet your needs

Philippians 4:19

Psalm 23:1

Take care of you and

your children

Psalm 68:5

Never leave or

forsake you

Deuteronomy 31:6

Be a Husband to you

Isaiah 54:5

Never Alone

BIBLE STUDY PASSAGE: 1 KINGS 17:8-16

God is in his holy Temple. He is a father to orphans, and he defends the widows.

PSALM 68:5

I worry that my son isn't around enough men. He needs a father figure.

I worry all the time about my kids, but sometimes I get so lonely and discouraged myself.

Some of my married friends don't include me like they used to; do they think I'm trying to steal their husbands?

There is no way to get around the fact that divorce creates a new set of challenges for a mother, which include her own feelings of hurt, grief, and guilt, plus the worry of how the children will handle the circumstances and details of mommy and daddy not being together.

The good news is that God is loving and gracious; He is kind and forgiving; He always stands up for the "underdog." So if you or your children feel just a little bit lost right now, be reminded that God declares: "He is a father to orphans, and he defends the widows" (Psalm 68:5).

Some other important reminders include—

On the day I called to
you, you answered me.
You made me strong
and brave.
Psalm 138:3

- You don't have to be married to be a complete person—
  you have what it takes to raise great kids. As one who is
  loved and restored by Jesus Christ, remember you have
  "everything we need to live and to serve God" (2 Peter 1:3).
- Pray that God will send "helpers" into your life to help
  you raise your kids. It's great to be strong and independent,
  and yet throughout the Bible we are told that we really
  do need each other. In Galatians 6:2, Paul reminds us to
  "bear one another's burdens" (NKJV). Pray that someone
  will help meet needs in your life.
- Don't feel guilty if you can't give your children "everything"
  every other kid has. "The important thing is faith—the
  kind of faith that works through love" (Galatians 5:6). If your
  children know they are loved, they have what really matters.
- God can work out anything and everything for good
  (Romans 8:28). No, divorce isn't God's best plan for
  anyone's life. But God can turn even tragedy into
  triumph. ➤

defends the widows" (Psalm 68:5).

Some other important reminders include—

On the day I called to
you, you answered me.
You made me strong
and brave.
Psalm 138:3

- You don't have to be married to be a complete person—
  you have what it takes to raise great kids. As one who is
  loved and restored by Jesus Christ, remember you have
  "everything we need to live and to serve God" (2 Peter 1:3).
- Pray that God will send "helpers" into your life to help
  you raise your kids. It's great to be strong and independent,
  and yet throughout the Bible we are told that we really
  do need each other. In Galatians 6:2, Paul reminds us to
  "bear one another's burdens" (NKJV). Pray that someone
  will help meet needs in your life.
- Don't feel guilty if you can't give your children "everything"
  every other kid has. "The important thing is faith—the
  kind of faith that works through love" (Galatians 5:6). If your
  children know they are loved, they have what really matters.
- God can work out anything and everything for good
  (Romans 8:28). No, divorce isn't God's best plan for
  anyone's life. But God can turn even tragedy into
  triumph. ➤

223

REAL LIFE

Happy Mother's Day

MICHELLE ORR

I am blessed to be the mom of two wonderful kids. I really do have every reason to celebrate every Mother's Day. But I know that second Sunday in May is a bit uncomfortable for my kids, as are most holidays, because "Dad" is not there to take them shopping and get that special card or gift. It's just one of the many tricky situations a single parent faces when holidays approach.

I've tried to make sure my kids understand that homemade things and gifts from the heart are the most meaningful gifts, but I can tell it still doesn't seem like quite enough for them at times. Who can blame them when commercials and newspaper ads scream to everyone that you "must" get Mom a really special gift of new clothes or fancy jewelry or sophisticated appliances?

So, to teach my kids what really matters on holidays, I started a tradition of going to my favorite restaurant with my children every Mother's Day for lunch. To some, it may seem a bit awkward for me to buy my own Mother's Day lunch, but it helps my kids feel like we're celebrating. I want them to grow up knowing that a single parent home is just as much a family as any other. I also want them to realize that I feel privileged to be their mother. Mother's Day is my day to be thankful to God for blessing me with children.

My kids have responded, and the Lord has made my somewhat unorthodox Mother's Days wonderfully special.

One year, my son announced that I didn't have to pay him as usual for mowing the lawn, the only chore for which he was paid, because that was my Mother's Day gift. The year my daughter was seven, she gave me a special "gift" for Mother's Day by saying, "You are the best mom in the whole world."

I teased her a bit by responding, "How do you know? You don't know all the moms in the world." She looked at me, a little stunned and puzzled. Then a look of determination crossed her face as she replied, "I just KNOW. You are my mom and I know you the best! So that is enough for me to know you're the best mom in the world." She continued as she wrapped her arms around my neck, "I'm sure of it!"

I returned the hug and apologized for teasing her. I thanked her for the very precious gift she gave me at that moment. How I hope she will say the same thing when she's seventeen! If she does, then I will receive a much more valuable gift than any store could sell for Mother's Day. ➤

ACTION STEP

HOW OFTEN DO YOU PRAY FOR YOUR CHILDREN? AS YOU ENDEAVOR TO MAKE SURE YOUR KIDS HAVE EVERYTHING THEY NEED, THE BEST WAY TO START IS BY GOING TO THEIR HEAVENLY FATHER. PRAY INTENSELY FOR YOUR CHILDREN EVERY NIGHT THIS WEEK—ASK GOD TO BE BESIDE THEM EACH DAY, GUIDING THEIR LIVES, MEETING THEIR NEEDS, AND PRESERVING THEIR SPIRITS. SOMETIME DURING THE WEEK, WRITE A SMALL NOTE TO YOUR CHILDREN THAT SIMPLY SAYS, "I'M PRAYING FOR YOU," AND TUCK IT IN THEIR SHOE OR LUNCHBOX.

PRAYER

O God, thank You for being a Father to me and my kids!

SIMPLICITY

LIFE IS BUSY AND CHALLENGING, BUT SOME OF THE PRESSURE WE EXPERIENCE COMES FROM OUR OWN UNREALISTIC SELF-EXPECTATIONS.

As children grow, they may not remember that you cooked a five-star meal every night or hosted an elaborate victory party for the entire Little League team, but they will remember that you listened to them over dinner and cheered their name as they slid into home.

ANONYMOUS

 To Think About

- Do you tend to feel pressure more from external or internal sources?
- Do you feel like more is required of you than is humanly possible to fulfill?
- Are you as compassionate with yourself as you are with others?

LESSON FOR LIFE

First Things First

BIBLE STUDY PASSAGE: LUKE 10:38-42

God will:

But Martha was busy with all the work to be done. She
Use and reward even
went in and said, "Lord, don't you care that my sister has
your smallest gifts
left me alone to do all the work? Tell her to help me."

of love

LUKE 10:40

Mark 12:43

Abundantly bless you
       Have you ever found yourself in a situation of being so
and enable you to
responsible, so dutiful, so correct in your religious practice that
bless others
you lost your joy of knowing God?
2 Corinthians 9:8
       In the famous parable of the lost son (Luke 15:11-32), a
young man rejects his father's teachings and authority,
demands his inheritance, and heads for a distant land where
Comfort your anxieties
he squanders his financial and moral wealth. The loving father
Psalm 94:19
never gives up on this prodigal, and when his young son does
come to his senses and ashamedly returns home, he welcomes
him with open arms. He honors him with a feast, a party, a
special cloak, and a golden ring. The older brother, who has
faithfully stood by his father's side this whole time, is enraged
that the prodigal should receive such a welcome. The father
sadly reminds his older son that you don't have to work in a pig

sty like his younger brother did to have a piggy attitude. Both sons learn about forgiveness and reconciliation from the love of their father.

In our study passage, we discover that Martha, much like the older brother, holds deep resentment toward a younger sibling. No, Mary is not immoral and rebellious, but she certainly doesn't have Martha's sense of responsibility. She leaves the dishes and chores to her sister so that she can sit at Jesus' feet. Wouldn't you feel a little resentful, too?

Jesus' answer to Martha's demand that He tell Mary to get busy is: "Martha, Martha, you are worried and upset about many things. Only one thing is important. Mary has chosen the better thing, and it will never be taken away from her" (vv. 41-42).

Is Jesus' point that we not care for the maintenance of our homes and families? Of course not. But He does remind us that the heart of our faith, our reason for living, is to love and worship God. Nothing else comes first! ➤

Life is more than food, and the body is more than clothes. Look at the birds. They don't plant or harvest, they don't have storerooms or barns, but God feeds them. And you are worth much more than birds.
Luke 12:23-24

REAL LIFE

Gourmet Snack-Baking Moms Need Not Apply

HEATHER LYNN IVESTER

At long last, it was my turn to bring halftime treats for our Saturday morning cheerleading squad. My seven-year-old daughter was so excited.

"What are you going to make, Mom?" she asked me early in the week.

"Oh, you don't worry about it. I'll whip up something fun and delicious!" I assured her.

When I'd signed up only a few weeks before, I imagined the mouth-watering frenzy my snacks would create. Oh, those poor mothers who only dashed out to the grocery store to pick up juice boxes and packaged munchies. Not me—no sirree! I would show them all.

I knew when my turn came, I'd leisurely browse through my vast (rarely opened) collection of wedding-gift cookbooks and choose the perfect, show-stopping treat, some little goodie loaded with nutrients to please the other parents, yet tasty enough to delight the girls.

My mind raced. Maybe I could create a snack shaped like an animal. Or a cartoon character. Better yet, something with a cheerleading theme—a megaphone or mini pom-poms. I couldn't wait until it was my turn to impress.

But something happened the week of my grand bake-off. I don't know what. Maybe it was the Cub Scout banquet, the nine loads of laundry, the missing library book, the science project forgotten until the night before, the newly scribbled-on family room wall.... Whatever it was, I completely forgot about the gourmet snack.

When we arrived in the gym, my heart sank. There stood ten smartly-dressed cheerleaders, eager for my forthcoming halftime delight.

I felt terrible. I was sure that every ballplayer and cheerleader and parent was staring at me. In my mind's eye, they tsked and found me guilty as charged: the mom with the best intentions, but the worst follow-through.

Actually, everyone was very understanding—especially the other moms. Store-bought snack cakes saved the day, but I was still disappointed in myself.

Once again, my pride had prevailed. In my zeal to outdo everyone, I'd failed to keep my to-do list simple. "Clothe yourselves with humility toward one another," I remembered (1 Peter 5:5). Yet I could think of a lot cuter outfits I'd rather wear than humility! As I wallowed in my disappointment, a woman walked over and handed me a flier.

"Would you like to join our prayer team?" she asked. "We're committing to pray every day for the spiritual growth of our basketball players and cheerleaders."

I felt my guilty emotions unwind from around my heart. "I'd love to!" I told her.

God met me that day as I sat in the stands, dwelling on my guilt as a cookie-baking failure. He showed me that anything I can do to help serve others is appreciated in His sight. Maybe one day I'll be the kind of grandmother who lovingly rolls out sugar cookies with her grandkids. For now, store-bought specials delivered with love and prayer will do just fine. ➤

ACTION STEP

ARE YOU EXPERIENCING THE JOY OF THE LORD IN YOUR LIFE RIGHT NOW? DOES LOVING GOD COME FIRST? THE NEXT TIME YOU FEEL OVERWHELMED BY THE VARIOUS DEMANDS IN YOUR LIFE, ACT COUNTER-INTUITIVELY BY STOPPING RIGHT THAT SECOND AND TAKING A MOMENT TO PRAISE AND WORSHIP YOUR LOVING HEAVENLY FATHER.

PRAYER

Turn my heart and mind to You right now, O God, my kind and gracious Lord. I put You before all other relationships, all other tasks.

SMALL MIRACLES

GOD'S LOVING CARE EXTENDS
TO EVERY DETAIL OF OUR LIVES.

I am graven on the palms of His hands. I am never out of His mind. All my knowledge of Him depends on His sustained initiative in knowing me. I know Him, because He first knew me, and continues to know me. He knows me as a friend, One who loves me; and there is no moment when His eye is off me, or His attention distracted from me, and no moment, therefore, when His care falters.

J.I. PACKER

 ## TO THINK ABOUT

- Have you ever experienced an incredible moment when you just knew God was doing something special just for you?
- Do you believe in miracles and divine intervention in your life?
- Do you go throughout your day with a sense of God's love for you?

LESSON FOR LIFE

Promises

God will:

Meet all your needs
Luke 12:31
1 Timothy 6:17

Give you the desires
of your heart
Psalm 37:4

Take care of the
details of your life
1 Peter 5:7

Tender Mercies

BIBLE STUDY PASSAGE: JEREMIAH 31:1-20

Let us, then, feel very sure that we can come before God's throne where there is grace. There we can receive mercy and grace to help us when we need it.

HEBREWS 4:16

When we get to the end of our own strength, realizing that we need God to make it in life and keep our souls tender and true, it's good to remember—

- God sent a rainbow to Noah as a symbol that His love for man would never waver (Genesis 9:14-15).
- God spoke to Moses in a burning bush (Exodus 3:2-6) and parted the waters of the sea with His breath to provide deliverance (Exodus 14:21).
- God allowed a young shepherd boy to conquer a mighty warrior with only a sling shot and a single stone (1 Samuel 17:49).
- Jesus healed a blind man (Mark 8:22-25), a person with leprosy (Matthew 8:2-3), a man who had never walked

(Matthew 9:2-7), and even raised a young girl from death to life (Luke 8:51-55).

- The Holy Spirit came upon the followers of Jesus so they could proclaim God's love in languages they'd never spoken before (Acts 2:4-8).

Peter instructed his persecuted flock to "give all your worries to him, because he cares about you" (1 Peter 5:7). He rightly expected that his readers would find comfort in knowing that an all-powerful God cares about the details of their lives.

God is still at work in our world today—and in your life. Sometimes all we need is to open our eyes to see His tender mercies in our lives. As you face each day's responsibilities and challenges, be on the lookout for serendipitous blessings from God and for ways to point those blessings out to your children. ➤

Even though you are bad, you know how to give good gifts to your children. How much more your heavenly Father will give good things to those who ask him!

Matthew 7:11

REAL LIFE

Traveling with Rainbows and a Prayer

KATHRYN LAY

We'd been planning this nine-day vacation for over a year. Our daughter, ten, had never left Texas other than an afternoon trip to Oklahoma one Sunday.

But now we were taking a long journey through the Deep South. Michelle could talk of nothing else for weeks. When the day came, we woke up at 4 A.M., packed our van to the brim, and headed out into the darkened streets. Miles whizzed by, and suddenly we were in Louisiana.

Before we knew it we were in Mississippi, staring at the Mississippi River.

Then the rain hit. It rained from Vicksburg to Biloxi. It wasn't long before we learned of Tropical Depression Allison sitting along the Texas Gulf Coast.

Together, we prayed for our long-awaited and needed vacation. We'd spent the last several years ministering to refugees and immigrants. That year had been especially busy and we needed this time of fun.

The clouds drifted away the first day as we toured a historical lighthouse. They returned just an hour after our first day of tourism stopped. Every day, we were amazed at how the rain stopped, never interfering with our plans, yet started again when we'd finished our tourist activities for the day.

Every night Michelle prayed for the rain to end. Somewhere, someone else was praying for the much-needed rain for this area to continue. And yet, both prayers were answered.

On the day we were to drive through Alabama and then on to Pensacola, Florida, to the beach, Michelle couldn't contain her excitement. Two more states and her first chance to swim in blue-green water and play on a white sandy beach.

It rained all the way to Florida. At the visitor center, we were told the red flags were up. No swimming. The water looked brown, not green.

We prayed for God's mercy as we sat down to lunch.

As we left the restaurant, we walked out into sunshine. We drove across the bridge to Pensacola Beach for an incredible afternoon of swimming in emerald water, burying one another in the sand, and marveling at the beauty of it all.

Our last day's tour was for me. A trip on a shrimp boat. It had been canceled all week due to rain. Yet, that Sunday, the clouds parted as we boarded the boat. It was all I'd hoped for—research information for a book and the thrill of watching two dolphins swim alongside the boat.

As we pulled into dock, the rain came down lightly. It didn't hit hard until we were safely inside a restaurant.

Even if God hadn't answered our prayers for sun, the wonderful conversation and stress-free travel would be evidence enough of His loving provision. But those beautiful rays of warm sunshine that streamed down just when we needed them—how incredible that the God of the universe would care so much about our vacation.

And as we looked over the gulf to say goodbye, a huge rainbow cut across the sky. →

ACTION STEP

ONE OF THE KEY WORDS IN THE BIBLE IS "REMEMBER." WE ARE TO REMEMBER GOD'S WORKS, HIS MERCY, HIS FAITHFULNESS. SOMETIMES WE FORGET ALL GOD HAS DONE FOR US.

FIND SOME TIME TO WRITE DOWN—

- WHAT YOUR LIFE WAS LIKE BEFORE YOU ENCOUNTERED GOD.
- WHAT GOD DID TO DELIVER YOU FROM "SLAVERY" IN YOUR LIFE.
- THE GRACIOUS DEEDS THE LORD HAS DONE FOR YOU SINCE YOU'VE BEEN WALKING WITH HIM.

TUCK YOUR "STORY" INTO YOUR BIBLE, AND LOOK AT IT AGAIN FROM TIME TO TIME. THIS MIGHT ALSO BE A GREAT TIME TO START A SPIRITUAL JOURNAL IF YOU HAVEN'T ALREADY DONE SO—A DAY-TO-DAY RECORD OF YOUR LIFE WITH GOD.

PRAYER

Dear Heavenly Father, thank You that being Your child means seeing Your comfort and provision in every detail of my life. Thank You for Your goodness.

LEAVING A LEGACY

AS WE COMMIT OUR PARENTING
EFFORTS TO THE LORD, HE GIVES US
THE GRACE AND ABILITY TO BLESS
OUR CHILDREN NOW AND IN THE FUTURE.

*There are two lasting bequests we can give
our children. One is roots. The other is wings.*

HODDING CARTER JR

To Think About

- Are there people from your family who have bequeathed to you a legacy of faith in God?
- What are some family treasures that you want to pass on to your children?
- What are the keys to passing on a godly heritage?

LESSON FOR LIFE

Promises

God will:

Bless your children and
grandchildren through
your godly life
Proverbs 12:7

Crown your efforts
with success
Proverbs 16:3

Make you more
like Christ
Romans 8:29

Be with your family
Isaiah 59:21

Train Up a Child

BIBLE STUDY PASSAGE: DEUTERONOMY 6:19

*We will not keep them from our children; we will tell
those who come later about the praises of the Lord. We
will tell about his power and the miracles he has done.*

PSALM 78:4

After the children of Israel were delivered from slavery in
Egypt, had passed through the long, arduous journey of the
wilderness, and were poised to move into the Promised Land, a
great challenge was given to the parents that would bless not
only their own lives, but also the lives of their children and
grandchildren.

- **Challenge #1**: Be obedient—"Obey all his rules and
  commands I give you so that you will live a long time"
  (Deuteronomy 6:1-2). There are no shortcuts on teaching
  the most important lessons in life—to raise obedient kids,
  we must set an example of obedience.
- **Challenge #2**: Pursue God's truth—"Listen, Israel, and
  carefully obey these laws. Then all will go well for you"

(6:3-4). As you pursue truth by honoring God and His Word, you set your children up to be a light in a society that celebrates moral relativism.

- **Challenge #3**: Love God—"Love the Lord your God with all your heart, all your soul, and all your strength" (6:5-6). Raising great kids is really about being who God wants us to be. Do your kids know how much you love God?
- **Challenge #4**: Teach God's Word—"Teach them to your children, and talk about them when you sit at home and walk along the road, when you lie down and when you get up" (6:7-9). Handing biblical principles down to the next generation seems like a huge task—but it begins with simple, everyday conversations between parents and kids.
- **Challenge #5**: Don't follow false gods—"Do not forget the Lord, who brought you out of the land of Egypt where you were slaves" (6:10-19). Even 5,000 years later, we are still faced with the temptation to follow false gods—gods of materialism and pleasure and success. Your children need to see a parent who is faithful to the one true God!

Raising children certainly isn't easy. But with time, patience, humility, and a complete trust in God, you can bless your children now and all the days of their lives. ➡

We have around us many people whose lives tell us what faith means. So let us run the race that is before us and never give up.

Hebrews 12:1

REAL LIFE

Sarah's Prayers

ELAINE INGALLS HOGG

I only met her a few times, but she had a tremendous influence on my life. My great-grandmother, Sarah Maude Green, worked hard to keep the home fires burning. Her husband left her alone for weeks at a time while he sailed around the world delivering goods to various foreign ports. Their humble home, the black wood stove in the kitchen, and the starched white doilies under the oil lamps are all part of my early childhood memories. In her lifetime, Sarah rarely left her home except for a quiet walk on the beach or to follow the dirt path that led to the church in the middle of the village.

Unfortunately, she died before my fifth birthday, so for a number of years she was only a name in a long list of relatives. During my adult years, I often found myself recalling her patient walk as she shuffled her arthritic figure across the linoleum floor and the hours she spent seated in her pillow-laden chair by the window, contentedly reading her Bible. Family members told me she had gone through many trials, yet I remembered only the air of graciousness she displayed at the end of her life. What gave her so much peace?

When my great-aunt died, I asked for a blue toffee tin that used to be in Sarah's home. To most, its value was negligible, for it contained nothing but a few scraps of paper, old newspaper clippings, and a few old buttons.

But among the yellowed clippings I found treasures, things my great-aunt had saved as a tribute to a godly lady. Like the words a neighbor wrote in loving memory, all because as a young woman, Sarah had decided to make her life count for God: "She was very faithful in the walk with her Lord. Although confined to her home in the latter years of her life, she was always cheerful and happy. A great inspiration to all who came to see her."

In her small, neat handwriting on the back of a faded church envelope, Sarah had penned:

To my children—

I leave this old book as the best heritage I can give. Study it carefully and you will find the way to peace and righteousness and happiness as I have done. If there is ever anything wrong with your lives, come back to this book as if it were a looking glass and it will clearly show you what is the matter. And when you are lost in the world, it will guide you home.

Mother

I never heard her speak more than a few kind words, and she died more than fifty years ago, but Sarah taught me that with God's help, one person can make a difference in the lives of generations to come. ➤

ACTION STEP

IF YOU DON'T HAVE A REGULAR BIBLE STORY AND PRAYER TIME WITH YOUR CHILDREN EACH DAY, NOW IS A GREAT TIME TO BEGIN. FOR YOUNG CHILDREN, THERE ARE MANY COLORFUL AND AGE-APPROPRIATE BIBLE STORY BOOKS. THERE ARE MANY DEVOTIONALS FOR TEENS, TOO. WHATEVER WORKS FOR YOUR FAMILY, FIND A WAY TO INTERACT WITH YOUR KIDS, EVEN IF IT'S ONLY POSTING A VERSE-OF-THE-DAY ON YOUR REFRIGERATOR.

PRAYER

Dear Heavenly Father, help me remember today that You've given me an awesome responsibility and opportunity to teach my kids about You—the same opportunity they'll have with their kids. Help me make the most of each day, Lord.

THE JOY OF SALVATION

EXPERIENCING GOD'S REDEMPTION
IN OUR LIVES IS CAUSE FOR GREAT JOY.

*In Christ we have a love that can never be fathomed, a life that
can never die, a peace that can never be understood, a rest that can
never be disturbed, a joy that can never be diminished, a hope that can
never be disappointed, a glory that can never be clouded, a light that can
never be darkened, and a spiritual resource that can never be exhausted.*

ANONYMOUS

TO THINK ABOUT

- How did you first experience God's salvation?
- In what areas of your life have you best experienced being redeemed?
- What does salvation mean for day-to-day living?

LESSON FOR LIFE

PROMISES

God will...

Save those who

call to Him

Romans 10:13

Forget your sins

Isaiah 43:25

Bring you to himself

Colossians 1:22

Bring you joy in

your salvation

Isaiah 12:3

A Bigger Heart

BIBLE STUDY PASSAGE: LUKE 19:1-10

The Father has loved us so much that we are called children of God. And we really are his children.

1 JOHN 3:1

If you grew up attending church, maybe you remember singing a song about a small man named Zacchaeus: *Zacchaeus was a wee little man, a wee little man was he. So he climbed up in a sycamore tree for the Lord he wanted to see.*

We don't know a lot about Zacchaeus' background, though we do know he was a small man—but not just because of his height. Like the Grinch from Dr. Seuss, what was truly small was his heart. A corrupt tax collector, he stole from his own people on behalf of the Romans, and as a result, the people despised him and he despised them.

But apparently, deep in his soul, Zacchaeus wanted something more—something bigger—in his life. He didn't want more money. He wanted to love and to be loved.

That all became possible when Jesus entered his life.

He opened his home to Jesus—and to those he once

despised. And unlike the rich young ruler who loved money more than people, Zacchaeus also opened his pocketbook and paid back even more than he had stolen. This "wee" little man is still the model of repentance today.

An encounter with Jesus brings a number of changes to our lives—

- Peace: "Let the peace that Christ gives control your thinking, because you were all called together in one body to have peace" (Colossians 3:15).
- A new heart: "If anyone is in Christ, he is a new creation" (2 Corinthians 5:17).
- Love for others: "We have heard about the faith you have in Christ Jesus and the love you have for all of God's people" (Colossians 1:4).
- A vibrant joy: "Being with you will fill me with joy" (Acts 2:28).
- Deep and sustaining strength: "I can do all things through Christ, because he gives me strength" (Philippians 4:13).

Celebrate! "You who were far away from God are brought near through the blood of Christ's death" (Ephesians 2:13). ➡

Thanks be to God for his gift that is too wonderful for words.

2 Corinthians 9:15

 # REAL LIFE

Something More

ELIZABETH CONNOR

When my neighbor invited me to start attending a Bible study with her, I experienced the strangest jumble of emotions.

I had been raised to attend church up through age twelve, and even went through a service to confirm my salvation. I was definitely raised to be a "good girl." My parents were probably the strictest in the neighborhood. My husband still says that meeting my dad was the most intimidating experience of his life. That's quite a confession from an ex-football player turned corporate veep who doesn't look like anything would scare him.

But despite a good, solid upbringing and wonderful parents with a strong faith, I was never raised to experience Jesus inside of me. So when the other ladies at this Bible study, whom I respected and liked a lot, started talking about forgiveness, prayer, and really getting to know God, I was a little bit confused.

I came to realize that I needed something more in my spiritual life. Faith for me had been about just going to church and mindlessly singing hymns. The rest of the week, I felt good about myself for going to church, but didn't give much thought to spiritual matters. I wanted something fresh deep in my heart.

One day after Bible study, I prayed the sinner's prayer with two of the ladies and really felt like something new and joyful—and yes, a little strange—had happened inside me.

One of the ladies took me under her wing and discipled me. I'd never known there was a verb for "disciple." My husband teased me that I was becoming a religious nut because I went to my weekly women's Bible study and also met regularly with this woman. But apparently he was ready for something more, too. To my amazement—and I was scared to death to bring it up—he was ready to try a new church. Before long, he'd gotten saved, too. Now I call him a nut because he gets up early almost every Saturday to go to a men's prayer breakfast. At least that's where he tells me he's going.

The greatest joy of my life was when I had the privilege to pray a prayer of salvation with my daughters, ages seven and eleven. They go to church and Sunday school, but we have our own little ladies Bible study each week. I love it.

I am working on my parents right now. I will always believe God made me who I am because of their love and care. I don't come on too strong about getting "saved," because my dad reminds me he already is. I think slowly but surely he and Mom are wanting something more in their hearts too.

What a privilege for me and my daughters to pray for them. ➤

ACTION STEP

WHEN WAS THE LAST TIME YOU PASSIONATELY WORSHIPED OUTSIDE OF A CHURCH SERVICE? SOMETIME IN THE NEXT WEEK, FIND SOME WORSHIP CDs AND PULL AWAY FOR A FEW MINUTES TO DO NOTHING BUT THANK AND WORSHIP GOD.

PRAYER

Lord God, thank You for saving me. Thank You for coming into my life. Today, I simply give You my love and thanks.

A PRAYER FOR YOUR SOUL

The most important soul matter, of course, is having a relationship with God. Everything in our lives—everything in our entire existence—has new, eternal meaning when we understand that God loves us and has made a way to save us through Jesus Christ. All of this may be new to you. If you'd like to know that you have a lasting relationship with God through Jesus, pray this prayer:

Heavenly Father, I come to You admitting that I am a sinner. I believe that Your Son, Jesus, died on the cross and rose from the dead to take away my sins. Jesus, I choose to follow You and ask that You fill me with the Holy Spirit so that I can understand more about You. Thank You for adopting me, and thank You that I am now a child of God. Amen.

READ THE BIBLE TO NURTURE YOUR SOUL

Your word I have hidden in my heart, That I might not sin against You.
PSALM 119:11 NKJV

We hope you have enjoyed this edition of Soul Matters.   We want to encourage you to continue taking care of your soul through regular church attendance, service to others, daily prayer and praise, reading other great inspirational books, and, of course, your own study of God's Word each day.

A couple of quick ideas that you might find helpful for studying God's Word include—

- Find a study Bible that fits your needs and is easy for you to understand.   Visit a Christian or general bookstore and you will discover a great variety of resources to help you really get into your Bible.
- Try different Bible study methods: One year, you can follow a daily reading plan that takes you through the entire Bible, or right now you might want to concentrate on just a few short books or chapters and spend focused time in memorizing and meditating on them. Be creative!
- Always begin your Bible reading with prayer: "God's word is alive and working and is sharper than a double-edged sword" (Hebrews 4:12). Ask God to speak to you through the pages of His Word.

Your soul will be nourished
as you spend time in His Word.

MEET WITH OTHERS TO NURTURE YOUR SOUL

*Let us not give up meeting together, as some are in
the habit of doing, but let us encourage one another.*

HEBREWS 10:25 NIV

We're confident that Soul Matters has been a source of encouragement and strength to your soul, and want to challenge you to share Soul Matters with others.

Why not consider using Soul Matters for a neighborhood Bible study or other small group setting, like Sunday school, accountability groups, and mentoring relationships?

IF YOU GO TO OUR WEBSITE AT
WWW.SOULMATTERSBOOKS.COM,
YOU WILL FIND FREE LEADER'S GUIDES
FOR TEN OF THE SOUL MATTERS
IN EACH OF THE EDITIONS.

Whether or not you use Soul Matters as a discussion starter, remember the importance of spending time with others in prayer and Bible study, in order to "help each other to show love and do good deeds" (Hebrews 10:24).

Acknowledgements

If you have enjoyed this book,
Hallmark would love
to hear from you.

Please send comments to

Book Feedback
2501 McGee, Mail Drop 215
Kansas City, MO 64141-6580

Or e-mail us at

booknotes@hallmark.com